*"Dear Mr. President . . ."*

Photo by Gene Lester

Ira Smith with photographs of some of the presidents under whom he served.

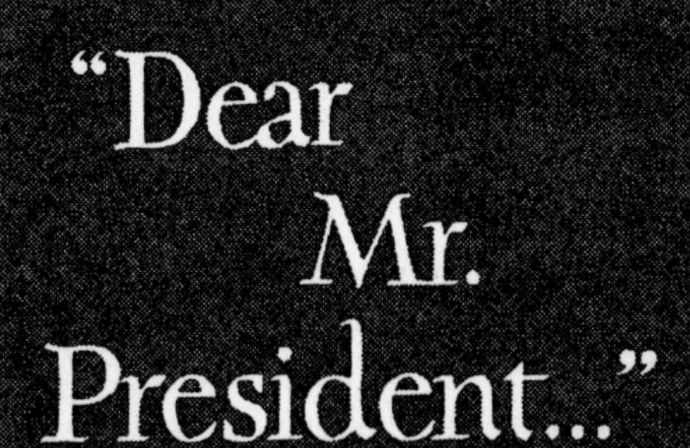


THE STORY OF
FIFTY YEARS
IN THE WHITE HOUSE
MAIL ROOM

By IRA R. T. SMITH with JOE ALEX MORRIS

JULIAN MESSNER INC. NEW YORK

PUBLISHED BY JULIAN MESSNER, INC.
8 WEST 40TH STREET, NEW YORK 18



[An abbreviated version of this book was serialized in The Saturday Evening Post under the title of *My Fifty Years In The White House.*]

PRINTED IN THE UNITED STATES OF AMERICA

To my efficient and loyal staff of assistants who helped me to whatever success I achieved in the office of Chief of Mails.

*"Dear Mr. President . . ."*

# *FOREWORD*

I WANT TO GET A WORD IN HERE BEFORE YOU START ON THIS book. For fifty-one years and three months I worked at the White House and thus I had a chance to see from that vantage point the development of our nation for about one-third of its actual history. It was a grand experience.

But I am not a historian, and I want to make one thing clear: This book is not a historical document about the White House and its occupants. If it is the history of great events that you're looking for, you'd save yourself a lot of effort by going fishing instead of reading this. You might have more fun, too.

My purpose in writing this book is to put down, while I still remember, some of my impressions of and reactions to events and people associated with the White House during the first half of the twentieth century. My connection with great events was too fragmentary to be of historical value. The history I will leave to the Jim Farleys, the Harold Ickeses and others whose advice was solicited by the Presidents.

I guess I always had my own ideas on how to run the Government, but since I wasn't asked for advice, I didn't give any. Good thing, too, because I was sure wrong a lot of times.

Ira R. T. Smith

March, 1949
Santa Barbara, California

# CHAPTER ONE

I SPENT FIFTY YEARS IN THE WHITE HOUSE READING THE President's mail, and let me tell you right now that even after you've opened a million letters addressed to somebody else you can still be curious about what's inside the next sealed envelope.

It's human nature, I suppose, to wonder what is in the other fellow's mail, especially if the other fellow happens to be the President of the United States. I have as much curiosity as the next one, but opening the White House mail just happened to be my job. It started out almost by chance as a part of the day's work back in the McKinley administration, but it grew into a career that meant a lot of excitement, some fun, and many headaches during the next half century.

You might as well know at the beginning that whenever you or many thousands of your fellow Americans sat down and wrote a friendly or an indignant or a worried letter to your President, it came to me instead of him. I or my assistants opened it, read it, and directed it toward either a suitable answer or the dark recesses of a filing cabinet. And from the days of President McKinley to the fourth year of President

Truman's administration, I opened a lot of letters that you wouldn't believe unless you saw them.

I guess that it is a natural result of our system of government that every citizen—as well as quite a few who aren't citizens—feels perfectly free to write to the President about his troubles or about his ideas of how the administration ought to be run. At least a great many do write such letters, and a few examples of what comes in the White House mail in addition to routine communications may give some idea of the problems presented.

A letter from a war veteran who wants help in finding a trunk that has been lost somewhere between Chicago and California. We found it.

A letter from a war widow seeking a pension and enclosing a sample of the ashes of her husband to prove he is dead. A clerk inadvertently opened it in front of an electric fan, and the evidence vanished.

A letter from a man who had written to the President on a political question, enclosing a stamp for reply, and had received his answer in a franked envelope. He angrily demands return of his stamp and that the President restore to the Government thousands of dollars which, he feels certain, have been "filched" in this manner.

A letter from a man in Iowa who for twenty-five years wrote regularly to the President demanding that his new method of scoring baseball games be universally adopted.

A letter, with money enclosed, requesting the President to grant a divorce.

Letters addressed to "The Onuble President," "The Great Promiser," "Calvin Coolidge—urgent—hasten—fly," "Too deer President," "Frankie Rassie Velt," "His Majesty of USA, Comrade and Buddy," "Pft—Phooy—Pres. Roosevelt," or "Mr. Presadene Frakline Rodserveet—if name spells wrong, please excuse." Many letters had no address other than a drawing of the President, and some were envelopes on which was written something like "May Jesus place this letter in the President's hands personally."

The gifts coming to the President covered an incredible range. A coyote sent to Teddy Roosevelt terrorized the White House offices when it escaped from its crate, but it turned out to be playful as a puppy. Other gifts that stick in my memory included two Nubian lions from Ethiopia, a large Alaskan eagle, alive and in such a combative mood that he struck at everybody who approached his cage; numerous horned toads; a Puerto Rican cow and calf for "the White House dairy"; a grain of rice with selections from the Koran written on it, which was lost when the package was opened and never recovered.

These, of course, are merely samples of the many thousands of things that come in the President's mail, but they give some idea of the tremendous problem the post office, as well as freight and express carriage, lays on the White House doorstep every day. It is both a heart-rending and an encouraging problem, because it presents a cross-section view of what is happening in our country, of how the people feel about things in general, and of their affection for—or bitterness toward—the Chief Executive. Almost every President has been deeply moved in times of great stress by the understanding and sympathetic letters that come from the little people, especially when they tell him of their personal problems.

Very few of them stop to think that the President cannot read even a small percentage of these letters if he intends to devote any of his time to the business of running the Government. They merely write the letters, put them in envelopes addressed to the White House, and drop them in the mailbox with implicit faith in the ability of the United States Post Office to deliver them to the man in whom they put their trust. I think I ought to say that, over the years, that trust has been fulfilled pretty well—not, of course, by the President himself, except in comparatively few cases, but as a result of the system set up to handle the White House mail as efficiently and as humanly as possible.

This system is not as involved as it might seem to the outsider, although in recent years it has required a large staff in the White House mail room itself. Basically, however, it is a distribution system designed to forward the letters to the government departments or bureaus that are especially equipped to handle each category. In other words, most people write to the President about problems that should be handled by the Department of Agriculture or the Bureau of Standards or the Patent Office or some similar branch of the Government. The work of the mail-room staff involves recording the receipt of such letters and forwarding them to the proper department for answers.

But in a place like the White House this job is a great deal more than mere routine, because nobody ever knows when a truckload of mail dumped on the doorstep will contain highly explosive matter—either a political bomb that must be handled with special care and an eye to the next election, or an actual bomb that must be turned over to the Secret Service. Either kind can cause a lot of trouble.

The political explosive, of course, is the most frequent, and I always had to keep my mind, and the minds of my staff, attuned to the latest ripples and currents of political developments in order to avoid missing the implications of what might look like an unimportant or routine letter but actually could turn out to be filled with political dynamite. It wasn't so difficult to know where to send letters for the proper answers as it was to decide which letters should be kept—usually for political purposes—at the White House for the personal attention of the President or his secretaries.

A mistake in connection with such letters might mean an affront to an important political personage, and a President can afford very few affronts to important politicians if he intends to keep on being President. I'll explain later how an unfortunate incident that was really nobody's fault had political repercussions all over the country during the early nineteen-thirties.

I had to make the decisions, and that is one reason why I always felt that the President of the United States and I were leading double lives. We had to if we were going to last very long in our White House jobs. During working hours, I put myself in the President's shoes and saw that every letter he received was sent to the right place for an answer. I made some mistakes, I suppose, but so did most of our Presidents, and I outlasted eight of them at the game. Maybe that was largely due to the fact that I didn't have to play the game all the time. In my off hours, I could go to the races or take my fishing boat down the Potomac or play a little poker, and be myself.

It was a lot tougher on the President. He had to have two distinct personalities—one for the public and one that was seen only when he relaxed with close personal friends or associates inside the walls of the White House. Sometimes that was quite a strain on everybody. Surprising sometimes, too.

There was Teddy Roosevelt, for instance. Mr. Roosevelt was a dominating, razzle-dazzle leader in public life, but he became as meek as a lamb when he joined his uninhibited family circle after a hard day of trust-busting at the office.

Woodrow Wilson was an incomparable logician, and a student of such broad vision that he often stumbled over the little facts of practical politics, but in private he liked to crouch at his old-fashioned typewriter and transcribe his own shorthand notes as if he were a $2400-a-year clerk.

Calvin Coolidge appeared to the voters as a shrewd, unruffled New Englander who kept government waste down and business profits up, but at home he rambled restlessly from cellar to attic fussing with petty details, and sometimes seething with suppressed irritability when he found something wrong.

Franklin D. Roosevelt in private was perhaps more like his public self than any other President I knew, because he never failed to present himself as the leading actor on whatever stage was available at the moment. He could make a grand gesture for the most lowly typist with as much enthusiasm as he gave to any historic occasion.

But of the nine Presidents under whom I served, from McKinley to Truman, the most puzzling and in some ways the most disliked during his term was William Howard Taft. This was not due to any lack of charm or intelligence on the part of Mr. Taft. To the public he was a fat, good-natured, smiling man whose administration was not especially good and not especially bad. But inside the White House he was unhappy; his feet hurt, he overate, and he often fell asleep and snored at his desk. I mention his administration in particular, however, because it was a turning point for the White House office staff.

Not long ago I was down on the bay in my boat one sunny afternoon when the fish were too lazy to bite and I was too lazy to care. I sat there with my hands holding a rod and my feet propped up on an icebox that Calvin Coolidge gave me, and I got to thinking back over what had happened in the White House in the last half century.

I thought: Well, there was a time when life was pretty simple even for the President. There were only a dozen of us on the White House staff at the turn of the century, and we knew each other's good and bad points. If we needed help or advice we could go to the President's secretary or to the President himself. We all felt we were part of one big family. Then in the days of Mr. Taft all that began to change. The change was due only in part to Mr. Taft, although the turning point came, as I will explain later, when his political advisers forced on him the first efficiency expert I had ever seen within shooting range. I was gun-shy for years after that experience.

But the real reason was that the business of the Presidency was growing up, and during World War I the staff expanded at a rapid rate. To the horror of us old-timers, even women came to work in the executive offices, and we had to quit messing around the locker room in our undershirts and give up our occasional dice and card games in the basement.

In the succeeding administrations our operations became so extended and so complex that the feeling of being "in the family" was never recaptured, except perhaps in a measure under Mr. Coolidge. Our jobs gained added excitement and interest, but by the nineteen-twenties we had become part of a big-scale executive operation.

It was President Hoover, with his engineering background, who brought the evolution to a scientific peak. He virtually engineered us into exile with the introduction of the multiple-secretary system that isolated him from White House personnel. A lot of people thought it was so efficient that it also isolated Mr. Hoover from the trend of public opinion, but that was not entirely true.

It remained for Franklin Roosevelt to complete the evolution by employing and expanding this system so skillfully that he created the illusion of his personal touch on everything connected with the White House.

Well, I was sitting there in my boat thinking about the different people who had lived in the White House and the vast changes that had come about in handling the mail, as well as in everything else, since I first went to work there in 1897. I thought that if I ever wrote about it I would have a hard time explaining some of the things that happened during those years. It wouldn't be easy, either, to explain to young people in this technological age how we got our work done when I was a young clerk handling President McKinley's mail and doing odd jobs around an office that I remember for its big ledgers with precise, handwritten entries, its cumbersome typewriters, and its clicking telegraph key.

It would be difficult, I thought, to make plain the attitude of the White House staff toward certain famous men and women and children—how we felt, for instance, when an exasperated clerk soundly spanked the naughty daughter of a President without knowing that her father was watching grimly from the doorway.

But I felt that the most difficult thing of all would be to explain how I managed to hang onto my job through almost thirteen administrations. That was no simple task in itself when you realize that I stayed put while six Republican and three Democratic Presidents moved in and out of the old mansion on Pennsylvania Avenue. I don't believe there is anybody else alive today who has held a comparable government post for so many years, who saw so many famous men and women come and go.

Let me be quick to say that my staying power should be attributed to peculiar circumstances as much as to any unusual talents of mine for the job that, in later years, was officially described as Chief of Mails. As Joe Louis once said when asked how he had managed to remain heavyweight champion for so long, "I was lucky." Yes, I was lucky, but I wasn't afraid of long hours when there was extra work to be done, and I had something else that seldom seems to be exactly harmful to a career in Washington—friends.

Let's be frank about it. I got my job in the first place

through political pull. In fact, there was plenty of political influence in my behalf at the White House but actually no specific job for me when my uncle persuaded President McKinley to hire me, and sometimes I had to scramble around to find enough work to keep them from catching on and sending me back to Ohio.

I don't feel that I was terribly ambitious. Like William Howard Taft, my sin was "an indisposition to labor as hard as I should." In defiance of American tradition, I never had any desire to be President, and seeing a few Presidents at close range merely confirmed my attitude. I just wanted to handle the White House mail.

I also wanted occasionally to see a good baseball game, to invest a few dollars in a crap game in the White House basement, and to find time to get a small bet down on the fifth race at Pimlico when the ponies were running. There's no reason to put that sentence in the past tense; that's what I still want. These inclinations, however, were often no help to me in my job, if I may state the circumstances in a restrained manner. In the early days I was the object of some severe lectures by the executive clerk. There were several of us in minor jobs who used to take advantage of dull afternoons to go down to the basement locker room, where it was dusty and quiet, spread out a blanket, and roll dice.

When executive clerk Rudolph Forster found us there he usually gave me the most severe dressing-down. One day, feeling that this was rank discrimination, I asked him why he always directed his sharpest remarks at me.

"Well," he replied, giving me a long stare, "whenever this

happens some of the boys may be here one time but not the next. You're here every time."

I had to admit that he was probably correct, but I didn't feel that it should really be held against me, because when there was work to be done I often kept on the job until midnight or later and regularly I worked all day Sunday.

There were a number of times, however, when my job was in jeopardy. One presidential secretary was fully determined to fire me, but changed his mind for a variety of reasons I will explain later. One President's wife wanted to punish the less sedate members of the staff, which naturally included me, for playing baseball on the lawn. And one President took office with the idea in mind that—because of a pre-election incident that was not my fault—I could be dispensed with. He was persuaded to change his mind later, and I worked for him longer than for any other President. Twelve years, in fact.

Actually, every time a new administration came in there was a period of political uncertainty that affected the entire staff, because new presidential secretaries are likely to want new personnel all down the line. And there are always political debts to be paid off. A large number of letters would come to each new President from political job-hunters who wanted to take my place as "postmaster" at the White House. These presumably deserving party workers seemed to go on the theory that there would be a new man in my job just as, in the olden times, the village post office got a new boss every time a national election brought a change in the party in power. Most such job-hunters could think of nothing easier that sorting a few letters for the presidential family and then sitting with feet on desk until the next mail came in.

It might have worked out that way, but it didn't. In the first place, there wasn't much time to loaf between truckloads of mail. I liked to get my feet up on the desk occasionally, but many times we worked until long after midnight, on Sundays, and on holidays trying to catch up with a flood of letters and packages. I figure that I have about seven years of overtime pay coming to me for all of my extra-hours work, but I never counted on getting it.

When I first went to work at the White House, President McKinley was getting an average of perhaps 100 letters a day, and there were frequent complaints that something would have to be done about such an avalanche of mail. As I grew familiar with the job, the mail grew by leaps and bounds. In President Hoover's time, the mail averaged about 800 a day, and during the New Deal it averaged about 8000 a day, with peak days on which we would go down under a count of 150,000 letters and parcels. We ceased to count the letters; we just lined them up and measured the length of each row. The mere physical handling of the mail required a staff that grew from one man—myself—to twenty-two regularly employed persons and in emergencies to seventy persons, including such volunteer helpers as Mrs. James Roosevelt, the President's daughter-in-law. She could go through a bag of mail with the best of them, and often did.

Fortunately, from my viewpoint, the mail always piled up in terrifying fashion with the advent of each new President. When the new President and his secretary got a glimpse of the thousands of letters arriving daily or stacked up awaiting an answer, they were likely to throw up their hands in helpless horror. Even if they had someone in mind for my job they were likely to shrug and say: "Well, let Ira Smith do it, at least for a while. He knows how."

So I would go ahead until they could "get somebody else," or until the backlog of letters had been cleared up, which usually took about six months. By that time I had either been accepted or something had happened to strengthen my position. When Woodrow Wilson came in, for instance, he was the first Democrat in the White House since my appointment, and I didn't feel particularly secure. They told me to go ahead, however, with stacks of mail that had been forwarded from his home and from the Democratic National Committee. It didn't hurt my standing when I found, in unopened letters containing campaign contributions, $65,000 that the Democrats didn't even know they had.

A lot of other unexpected things have been found in the White House mail in the last fifty years, including a few disguised but highly dangerous packages of explosives. None of the dangerous mail ever got close to the President and, with modern methods now in use, none of it ever will. But in a job like mine the possibility that you might come across something was always in the back of your mind, along with a huge mass of miscellaneous data concerning ways to recognize the mail from members of the President's family, the handwriting of important correspondents, the color of the envelopes used by personal friends, and odd postmarks that meant letters in which the Chief Executive would be personally interested.

After a while, a man handling mail of this nature develops a sort of sixth sense that makes it possible for him to work with great speed. I could tell almost by looking at them something about the contents of most of the letters and packages that came into the White House mail room. Especially if they were crank letters or dangerous packages.

In the old days, when we lacked any sort of scientific apparatus for examining the mail, it was up to me to guess whether a package was dangerous, unless it happened to be spotted by the post-office clerks before it was delivered to the White House. Since it was my neck that was at stake, I became accustomed to taking a good look at all packages before opening them or even before handling them. This became second nature with me, and the danger signs would automatically register in my mind as I looked over the day's deliveries. The lack of a return address was one thing I noted immediately, because that became a familiar clue to the crank letter or the dangerous package. Just as suspicious was a return address such as "John Brown, Podunk, Ohio," unless we happened to know such a person, because a crank is not likely to have much imagination in such matters.

If a package was particularly heavy for its size, it was likely to be laid aside for later examination and of course if it ticked, I frequently dumped it into a bucket of oil before opening it. I was always a reasonably cautious man, and that may help account for the lack of explosions around the White House mail room in my time there. I was fortunate, as well, because on a couple of occasions there were explosions of White House mail while it was still in the hands of the General Post Office.

Over the years we worked out methods of handling all mail, but it was always interesting to study the methods of correspondents who sought to avoid our precautions. I remember one envelope addressed to the President with the notation: "Very personal, if that means anything to a long-nosed secretary." And another that said: "Anyone opening this letter other than the President will be subject to a lawsuit." Sometimes the writers of letters that failed to reach the President would become so incensed that they would travel many miles to make a personal visit to the White House. Usually I had to try to pacify them. Some of them went away happy, but sometimes I needed police help to get rid of them or to prevent violence.

Other habitual correspondents resorted to all kinds of tricks, such as throwing letters into the President's automobile as he drove along the street, or enclosing a bribe in a letter with a plea to get it to the President. Occasionally expensive gifts accompanied the letters for the same purpose. Others tried to hand letters to the President's wife at public affairs, or to deliver them by hand to the front door of the White House. All of them ended up in the same place—the mail room.

And having reached the mail room, they became, of course, my responsibility. Sometimes it was a responsibility that couldn't be discharged to suit everybody, and I suppose I occasionally ruffled the feelings of important persons. Sometimes it took a bit of scheming and a bit of political pull to keep things going around the office, and not infrequently it was tough going, at that. Well, that was all right with me. As far back as I can remember to my boyhood in the California mountains I've had to be reasonably fast on my feet to get along. I've had to be pretty tough sometimes, too.

## CHAPTER TWO

I'VE SAID THAT I GOT MY JOB THROUGH POLITICAL PULL, SO I think I'd better explain about my Uncle John. He was my pull.

Uncle John was John N. Taylor, my mother's brother, and a man who had made his way up to become president of the huge Knowles, Taylor and Knowles potteries in East Liverpool, Ohio. His way may have been made a little less rugged when he married the boss's daughter, but that was in the best American tradition, and anyway my point is that he got to the top. He was a pillar of rock-ribbed Republicanism in the state, and that meant that he was on close terms with such fabulous characters as Mark Hanna, and of course William McKinley.

My uncle John made a big thing out of china plates and cups and saucers when the East Liverpool potteries were among the largest in the world, and his campaign contributions helped do big things for the Grand Old Party in Ohio, too. In fact, at one time he had a hand in a bit of financial aid to Mr. McKinley when times were tough, and he was naturally gratified when there came a day on which Mr. McKinley, pushed somewhat by Mark Hanna, moved into the White House.

These developments were important to me, too, because Uncle John had more or less looked after me from the time I was in my early 'teens. My father was William J. Smith, born on a farm near Midway, Pennsylvania. My grandfather Smith had made a good thing of several farms that he owned, and he gave one of them to each of his sons. Father took his, but he didn't want it. He wanted to be a preacher, and he was entranced by the famous evangelists of the day, including Moody and Sankey. He went to Pittsburgh and studied under a famous Presbyterian minister, Dr. Sylvester Scoville, and later he traveled the evangelistic trail. He never went to a theological seminary, but he became an ordained minister. He also met and married an Irish girl named Elizabeth Taylor.

My parents lived on the farm for a couple of years, and I was born there in 1875, and named for Ira D. Sankey, with Robert Taylor added on by Mother. When Father was offered the pastorate of the First Presbyterian Tabernacle at San Francisco, he turned the farm back to his father for cash and took off for the West. My mother and my baby sister Ethel and I followed as soon as he had made preparations for us. In San Francisco Father became known as the Sporting Parson, because he loved outdoor life and big-game hunting. Frequently he supplied deer and bear steaks for members of his congregation. Once he and Mother made a trip to the Hawaiian Islands, where they were entertained by island royalty and took part in exciting hunts for the small wild cattle that overran some of the islands.

Father was a big and handsome man, standing an inch over six feet and weighing about 190 pounds. His thick black hair was combed back from his forehead, and he had a full mustache that curled a trifle at the ends.

He was an excellent shot and a natural athlete. I have seen him jump completely over the dining-room table from a standing start. He spoke gravely and precisely, but he was a man who enjoyed a good time, especially in the outdoors.

His congregation had given him an unusual gun, which had three barrels. Two were shot-gun barrels and the third, which was underneath, was a rifle. One day when we were hunting I saw him line up two birds and bring down both of them with a shot from one barrel. As he fired, a large buck deer and a young buck got up from the brush near by and ran in different directions. He got both of them with the other two barrels.

When I was seven or eight years old, he sometimes took me with him to hunting camps in northern California. The little narrow-gauge railroad we traveled on followed a twisting, curving path into the mountains, sometimes almost doubling back on itself. It also ran very slowly, and more than once we got off on a curve and cut across the hillside to shoot some game, catching the train on the run again as it rounded the next loop in the track.

When I was about eight, my mother took us children—I now had a small brother named Ned—back to Ohio and Pennsylvania on a visit. In those days it took ten days to make the trip from California by train, and a dreary journey it was. While we were gone, Father became ill, and the doctors told him he ought to live in the mountains. He wrote us about it. He said that he had bought a ranch in the mountains above the Santa Ynez Valley in southern California, and that it would be ready for us when we got back.

We didn't go directly there, however. He met us at Duncan's Mills, above San Francisco, when we returned. He was thin and seemed restless, and when he had kissed each of us, he turned to Mother and said:

"Bessie, I've got to have a drink of whisky."

We all looked at him in pop-eyed fashion, except Mother, who may have realized that he was tired and sick, and that the long trip from Santa Ynez had done him no good.

"Will," she said, "don't you go in a saloon. People will talk. If you need a drink, just get a bottle of whisky and take it to our hotel room."

Father was not a drinking man, except for wine with his meals occasionally, but this time he had made up his mind that he needed a drink, and he wasn't going to resort to any subterfuge.

"No, ma'am," he said. "I need a drink and I'll be honest about it and have it at the bar."

He went into the saloon and leaned his long frame against the bar and had his drink. When he came back I asked him when we would get started for the ranch.

"Well, son," he replied, "we'll have to wait a few days. Things aren't quite ready there and we need some rest. Then we'll take the boat down to Santa Barbara."

A few days later we went down to Santa Barbara. That, Father explained, was as close to the ranch as the boat went. "Now we have to get the stage," he added. "This is the Wild West."

I thought it was fine. The stage was pulled by four lively horses and we jolted over a rocky, dusty road that wound slowly over San Marcos Pass. On beyond in the valley the road was frequently so full of ruts that we had to circle into the open fields to avoid getting stuck. It was fun to keep an eye peeled for Indians and stagecoach robbers. There weren't any highwaymen that day and there never had been any Indians, but it was still fun. We were all pretty tired by the end of the day and glad to see the town of Santa Ynez. We were really out in the wilds.

"Are we there now?" I asked Father after we had washed the top layer of dust off our faces. He grinned at me and said that we were just going to stop in Santa Ynez for the night, because that was as close to the ranch as the stage line went.

"Tomorrow," he went on, "we get some buckboards and a few pack mules and go up that way." He pointed toward the mountains. I looked at Mother. She had never lived in surroundings much more rugged than East Liverpool and San Francisco, and she was pretty busy with Ethel and Ned, but her eyes twinkled at me. She was game.

The next day we traveled slowly along the rough mountain road, climbing steadily. The buckboards bounced and the pack mules had to be prodded along. There was an occasional ranch house, but mostly there were just the woods and the mountains. About dusk we stopped. I couldn't see anything that looked like a ranch, but I didn't feel much like asking questions again.

Father explained, however, that we couldn't get to the ranch that night and that we would camp where we were.

"This is as close to the ranch as the road goes," he said. "Tomorrow we'll go on horseback. I've got some stone sledges to haul our goods on. It's only four miles up the trail."

It all seemed more than passing strange to me, but I was too tired to think about it and we settled down to sleep after a makeshift supper.

Next morning we loaded the pack mules and the stone sledges and started out over a trail that was too rough for anything with wheels. It was almost too rough in spots for the sledges, and often we had to hold up one side of a sledge while the mules pulled it uncertainly over a narrow rocky ledge.

I have no idea what was going through Mother's mind as we labored up that trail to the ranch in Cachuma canyon. She was a pretty, plump, and healthy young woman, not much more than five feet tall, and she was not the worrying kind. Her dark, red-tinged hair was long enough to reach below her waist, but she wore it twisted into knots on her head, usually without a hat. In the mountains she wore heavy bloomers that came below her knees and a dark skirt that barely covered the bloomers. Nothing ever seemed to faze her, then or later.

Perhaps she had known all along what we were heading for, or perhaps she was just one of those women who can take what comes, whether it's the wilderness or the White House.

Anyway she *did,* and it seemed to me that she was just about as much in character that day on the rocky trail as she was later among the gold braid and fancy gowns at a White House reception.

But somewhere along that trail I began to connect up what had happened and to guess that Father's illness was more serious than we had been told. Looking back at it now, I assume that he had suffered a nervous breakdown and that, at least part of the time, his actions were irrational. But then I realized it only vaguely, and Mother never let on that anything was wrong. Even with three small children on her hands, she could take it.

We came at last to the ranch, in a rugged canyon with a good stream running through it. Near the stream was a sturdy little storehouse and we stopped there first. Father showed us how well he had stocked it. He was quite proud of the cases of good wine, bottled olives, canned fruit (very rare in those days), and other luxury goods that were stacked high along the walls. There was plenty to last through the winter.

We walked on across the ranch. There were plenty of chickens and turkeys and milkcows. There was, in fact, just one thing that Father had neglected. There wasn't any house to live in. The foundation of a house had been started, but it would be months before it was finished. Meantime, there were two tents with wooden floors to shelter us—and the rainy season was coming on. There were stoves and beds in the tents and that night we went to sleep exhausted, worrying very little about tomorrow.

Well, we got along. There were times when Father was his old self and we hunted together. On one such occasion we walked about a mile up the mountain, where he shot a deer that bounded away up the trail and around a bend. We followed the trail of blood, polished the deer off, and hung it up on a tree to be picked up later.

Going back down the trail, Father walked in front. Just as he came to the bend he stopped abruptly, stepped back and fired his gun. A big mountain lion landed exactly where Father had been standing. It was very dead, having expired in mid-air with one bullet in its heart. Didn't even move after it hit the ground. Apparently the lion had been following the trail of blood left by the deer, and was so excited that it attacked the moment it saw us. It measured eight feet from nose to the tip of its tail and was about the biggest mountain lion I ever saw. I saw quite a few of them, too, because while we lived on the ranch they used to come down to the edge of the creek almost every night and try to make off with some of our turkeys or chickens. Sometimes they made a terrific racket.

There were not many hunting expeditions, however, in Cachuma canyon, because Father's health was failing rapidly and he became irritable and erratic. He lost his taste for ordinary food and spent much of his time planning and preparing delicacies, or sending me to town on horseback to bring him something that he thought might whet his appetite. I was kept so busy running his errands and working on the ranch that I often found myself falling asleep at meals or on horseback.

Finally he got some pigeons, and built a pigeon cote on a high pole. He remembered that he had enjoyed squab when he lived in the city and could get it properly prepared. About four o'clock one morning he woke me up and sent me out to the pigeon cote.

"Ira," he said, "I always like squab for breakfast. Will you climb up that pole and get me one?"

Weary, half-asleep, and numb, I climbed up the pole, and Father had squab for breakfast. He was a good cook, and it was probably better than he could have got under glass at the Hotel St. Francis. But almost every morning for weeks we repeated that scene before dawn. It became a sort of nightmare that went on endlessly and dreadfully, high up there in the mountain canyon—witnessed only by our sleepy dogs and occasionally a sulky wildcat.

Father also had purchased a lot of blooded stock for the ranch. We had horses, pigs, turkeys, and cattle, but they were not properly cared for and got wilder and wilder. Eventually, all of them were lost to the wilds, to the adjacent ranches, or to the animals in the forest.

Father's condition became steadily worse, and finally he had to go to a sanitarium near San Francisco, where he died in 1887. Mother went to San Francisco at the time of his death, leaving me alone on the ranch and parking my brother and sister with a family down in the Santa Ynez Valley.

I didn't mind being left alone, because I could take care of myself, but I didn't often see anybody because we were so far off the road. So I was surprised one day when a dirty and bearded character showed up at the ranch house.

"Hello, sonny," he said. "Where's your folks?"

I told him.

"You here alone, eh? . . . Well, I was just looking around for a place to stay. Maybe I could sleep in that cabin you got down on the creek. I guess that'll be okay, eh?"

"What are you doing here?" I asked him. He looked like a tough one to me.

"Oh, I got a job with the old guy across the hill. Herding his cattle. That cabin of yours is handy and I'll just sleep there. My name is Blood."

There wasn't much I could do about it. That night I locked myself in the house and then locked the door of my room, and I got out the biggest bear trap we had. It was so big you had to use a lever to open the jaws and set it. I got it set and put it under the only window of my room. Even then I didn't sleep well. Blood didn't look like a cattleman, and after I had watched him a few days I was pretty sure he was lying.

Then one day the sheriff rode up to the house and asked if I'd seen any strangers around. I told him about Blood and he said that was the man.

"Want him for robbing a stagecoach," he said. But when we went to the cabin Blood was gone. They caught him the next week at a town down in the valley, but I don't know what finally happened to him.

Not long after that I got to feeling lonesome, and one day I saddled a horse and rode down to the valley to see Ethel and Ned. I met them on the road before I got to the ranch house where they were staying. Both of them burst into tears when they saw me. They were dirty, and told me fearfully that they had been mistreated by the family that was supposed to be looking after them. I took them up on the horse and we rode back to the ranch.

We got along all right until a few nights later, when a terrific storm hit the canyon. The wind blew so hard that the house shook and we couldn't sleep. After a while we became badly frightened, and we got up in the middle of the night and started down the hill to a little cabin that was better protected from the wind. I carried Ned and held onto Ethel's hand, and I thought we were all three going to be blown off the side of the mountain. Just as we left the house, the whole roof blew off, and a big piece of it sailed a few feet over our heads. We ran madly to the cabin. Soon a heavy snowfall began.

The next day before daylight Mother arrived, leading a horse and carrying her little black-and-tan terrier. The evening before, she had called at the ranch where Ethel and Ned were supposed to be staying, and found them gone. The ranchers didn't know where they were, and didn't seem to care much. Mother borrowed a horse and, carrying the little dog, started the fifteen-mile ride to the ranch. About four miles from the ranch the dog jumped out of her arms, and after she had caught it again she couldn't get back on the horse. She walked the last four miles, only to find the roof blown off the house, the rooms covered with snow, and no children in sight. We were all three sound asleep when she found us in the cabin. For an Easterner, Mother certainly put up with some rough times in California.

The only schooling we had was when Mother had time to

teach us to read and write, and to work simple arithmetic problems and a little grammar. A few rough edges were knocked off by a sojourn in Ballard, where I attended the country school. Mother's brother John was getting along well in East Liverpool, Ohio, and in 1889 he decided to send me to the San Mateo Military School. I was a raw and independent kid by that time. I didn't care much for discipline, and I didn't stand in awe of my elders, or anyone else. The life I had been living on the ranch and on long hunting trips in the mountains failed to encourage respect for authority, but I was usually able to protect myself in the clinches.

When I first went to San Mateo, I didn't like the idea of being pushed around by the upperclass boys, and I let them know it. They decided to give the newcomer a lesson in discipline and, almost before I realized what was happening, they had me in an impromptu outdoor boxing match with the school champion. There wasn't any question in anybody's mind, including my own, that he was going to teach me to respect the upperclassmen by knocking my head off.

Since I couldn't get out of it, I put on the boxing gloves and approached him with as much confidence as I could muster. He obviously had decided to waste no time on me, and he uncorked his Sunday punch in the direction of my chin. It would have been a devastating blow except that as he swung, his foot slipped on some small stones and he started to fall. I saw what was happening and stepped in close and popped him square in the face as he went down. After that I didn't waste any time. I turned my back on him, shrugged my shoulders and took off the boxing gloves. I walked away as sedately and as rapidly as possible. Even then I knew a lucky break when I saw it.

In school I was ahead of my class in some things, but far behind in others. After a year and a half, however, I managed to get to the top of the honor list in everything except deportment.

My uncle John had been urging Mother to return to Ohio, and finally she made a trip there, leaving us children in the care of different families around Santa Ynez. My brother stayed with Mrs. Lyman, who owned a ranch not far from us. She was a vigorous and emphatic old girl who had had five husbands and was still going strong. She didn't want Ned to wear out his good clothes around the ranch, so she made him some strange costumes out of flour sacks. He looked like a freak, but he loved it, and later we had a tough time getting him back into ordinary clothes.

A remarkable old character with a flossy white beard and known all over the county as Uncle Davy Brown lived twenty miles over the mountain from Mrs. Lyman. Uncle Davy's leathery face had more wrinkles than a box of prunes, but he was a lively number, and I often visited with him for several days at a time. His cabin was a one-room affair with a door but no windows, and there was a lean-to where he did his cooking. The lean-to had swinging doors at each end, and when he wanted a fire he would haul in a long log the size of a tree, trim the branches, and put it on a sort of fireplace made of rocks in the center of the shed. He would then start a fire in the middle of the tree and keep pushing the ends together as the middle burned. It worked fine, and saved a lot of wood-chopping.

One night when I was sitting on a pyramid of logs covered with bearskins and listening to Uncle Davy's stories of the Mexican War we heard a squawking among the chickens roosting in a tree near the cabin.

"That varmint's back," Uncle Davy muttered, and he got down his muzzle-loading rifle. He handed me a lighted pine knot and told me to throw it over the cabin when he yelled. I threw it, making an arc of fire over the roof, and while the light lasted he shot a big mountain lion off a limb above the roof. I shall never forget the thump as it hit the roof and the scratching as it slithered off. In the meantime I had taken refuge in the cabin with the door tight shut. I still have one of the lion's claws.

Uncle Davy had a boy working for him, but they didn't get along, and he was always asking me to take over the job. Finally he told Mother that he would legally adopt me and make me his heir. He claimed he had two ranches and $25,000 in the bank, and he pointed out that he wasn't going to be around much longer, because he was then about ninety. Mother was planning to return to Ohio and she declined the offer. We rather doubted that the old duffer had any money. He didn't look it, and we thought he probably just wanted a boy to help on the ranch.

Once every week Uncle Davy got aboard a horse and rode down to the lazy, dusty little town of Ballard to buy a few supplies and see how civilization was getting along. His road went past Mrs. Lyman's ranch and he always stopped off there to get a meal and sometimes to stay overnight. One week he failed to show up on schedule. Mrs. Lyman saddled a horse and rode over to his ranch and found him pretty sick. She settled down to take care of him.

Years before that time Mother had agreed with Uncle John and had gathered us children together again and taken us back to East Liverpool. I went to high school there. I didn't get back to the Santa Ynez Valley for more than half a century, and when I did our ranch had reverted to the wilds. I went up to look it over one day and had a lot of trouble finding the spot where the house had been. A willow tree about two feet thick was growing where once we had the kitchen. Everything was changed except the mountains and Ballard. Both seemed to be just about the same. When I was reading a newspaper a few days later I came across a column that reprinted items from "Fifty Years Ago." One of the items said:

July 7, 1898

An estate valued at $30,000 has been left to the woman who took care of him in his old age by Uncle Davy Brown of Guadalupe. Two mules, Tom and Jinks, are to be cared for upon the ranch without work so long as either of them lives. The 30-year-old animals are to be kept in good condition with ample pasture. Declaring he had never been married, the deceased provided that any alleged widows or adopted children if proved authentic should receive $50.

Well, I thought, I finally got the end of the story. It was Mrs. Lyman, however, who got the dough.

# CHAPTER THREE

I WAS SITTING IN A SMALL POKER GAME ONE MARCH EVENING in 1897 at Wooster, Ohio, and holding three aces. The pot had just been worked up to an interesting size when my brother ran in with a telegram. I had been more or less expecting the telegram, but my hand trembled a bit as I carefully put down my cards and tore it open. It said

IF INTERESTED IN POSITION AT WHITE HOUSE $1200 PER ANNUM COME AS SOON AS POSSIBLE. UNCLE JOHN.

I left the three aces, a six, and a trey face down on the table and rushed home to get ready. It was a big break and a big salary for me, but it was more than that. It was the first time I had been able to put much faith in my family's long-standing belief that politics paid off. Uncle John had come through in the pinch. It was about time he got a break, too, because he had lately suffered some unkind blows. One had come a few years earlier when that man Grover Cleveland got into the White House and the Democrats put through a free-trade program. Those were sad days for Uncle John and a lot of other Republican industrialists.

Another blow came when I announced I would do almost anything in the world except go into Uncle John's pottery business. I had attended Wooster University (it is now Wooster College), pitched for the baseball team, learned not to draw to an inside straight, squired a few pretty girls around, and completed my course without arousing any outbursts of enthusiasm on the part of the university authorities. I had some vague idea that I would like to study law, but the truth is that I was not headed in any particular direction along life's highway. That meant that Uncle John had to worry about me as well as about Grover Cleveland, because nobody, including myself, could figure out exactly what I was fitted for in life. Mr. McKinley solved both problems by defeating the Democrats in the presidential election and inviting Uncle John to visit at the White House immediately after the inaugural ceremonies. He was still the President's guest when he sent the telegram telling me to hurry to Washington. Neither he nor Mr. McKinley had yet figured out what I was fitted for, but the President was willing to try.

My job, when I got to it, was in the executive offices, which were on the second floor of the White House proper. The office force of six clerks, a secretary, an assistant secretary, and an executive clerk was in two rooms across the hall from the presidential office, which adjoined the Lincoln Room. John Addison Porter, who was Mr. McKinley's first secretary, took an interest in me, but sometimes my green and probably dumb performances drove him into an outburst of temper.

My duties as a clerk were not very strenuous, and when the President was out of town I had plenty of free time. I was beginning to worry about the danger of my job vanishing into thin air when Porter decided that I should help Mrs. McKinley with her mail. She was a semi-invalid, a gentle and kindly woman, and I enjoyed working with her.

I put my best efforts into the job. Mrs. McKinley was pleased and I, unknowingly, had solved the problem of a career. A man named Joe Moss had been working in the presidential offices, and among other things he handled the President's mail when it was delivered, opening and sorting the letters and turning them over to Porter or one of the clerks. When Moss was transferred elsewhere, Porter looked around for someone to take over this thankless odd job and picked on me because I had handled Mrs. McKinley's mail. I heaved a sigh of relief when I was told the news. They had practically had to manufacture a job for me, but now I had it, and it was going to be fifty years before they could get me out of it.

When you think of the McKinley days you have to forget such things as radios, bubble gum, airplanes, and atom bombs. There weren't any. There were days of war at the turn of the century, but mostly these were days of tremendous economic expansion, of handsome carriages on the avenues, of waving plumes on ladies' hats and real bustles that in no way resembled the fashionable foolishness that came along fifty years later with something called the New Look. The railroads were sticking out shining steel fingers all over the West, and great financial empires rocked with the schemes of the James J. Hills, the Morgans, the Harrimans, and the Jacob Schiffs. There was a newfangled contraption called the Stanley Steamer, a horseless carriage that ran on steam generated by naphtha—providing it could find any road good enough to run on.

But these things, for the most part, touched the White House only pleasantly, or indirectly, or not at all. Except for the war, of course, and the Stanley Steamer, in which the President was persuaded to go for a trial spin at the speed of eighteen miles an hour. It was generally conceded that such speed was outrageous, and a foolish risk of the neck of the Chief Executive.

One of the first things I noticed about life in the White House—and it was still noticeable when I retired from my job—was the heavy load that the President personally is forced to carry. The nation has grown and expanded and become a highly complex civilization in the last century and a half. Yet in many ways the Presidency has remained almost unchanged since the days of George Washington, permitting a vast burden of pressures and duties to grow up that make it a killing job.

I would go into President McKinley's office and find him sadly eying a huge stack of commissions, including those of junior officers. He would shake his head unhappily, or he might hum a Methodist tune as if it would give him courage to face the task.

"Let's get busy," he would say after greeting me. I would hand him a commission from the pile, he would sign it, and then I would put it on a table to dry before it was returned to the department for mailing. This was necessary since each commission was made of sheepskin and could not be blotted. The President would hum harder and sign less happily as we worked through the pile, and soon all the desks in the office would be covered and I would start spreading the commissions out on the floor. By the time the first one signed was dry, the Chief Executive would be surrounded by an ocean of commissions that stopped all traffic and virtually all business.

"Something ought to be done about this," he would complain at intervals. "Somebody else ought to be able to sign these."

But it was a long time before the President was even partly relieved of a job that may have been necessary in George Washington's day, but not in the twentieth century. Even today, however, it is a duty that eats heavily into the President's time and strength.

I suppose that McKinley, Wilson, and Franklin Roosevelt, because they were war Presidents, felt the strain of office more acutely than the others I knew. I can never forget President McKinley's face when he stood in front of the White House and watched the boys who had fought in Cuba parade up Pennsylvania Avenue. The sickly color of their skin and the way they marched even when passing before the Commander-in-Chief told a story that the President already knew from countless cables and letters that I had passed on to him.

It was a sordid story of contractors who took big profits for supplying the Army with moldy hard tack and spoiled corned beef; of inadequate medical supplies for men stricken with malaria, typhoid, and dysentery; of death by disease and neglect far outweighing the toll among those who went into battle. Sometimes Mr. McKinley sat at his desk until long after midnight reading the letters and cables that disclosed this disgrace to the nation. The anger and disgust and sorrow that they brought him made his face gray and grim as he watched the parade of victory in which so many men could never march because of greed and inefficiency at home.

Mr. McKinley was, I suppose, the last of the old-style frock-coat presidents, but to me he was always a thoughtful friend. There was far more call in those days for the President to employ a personal approach in political affairs, and in this Mr. McKinley was unequaled. On one early occasion before he became President I saw him demonstrate his ability to handle any situation with unruffled friendliness. My family had a little summer camp in Ohio where Mr. McKinley was a guest on the occasion of a small fishing party. He didn't like summer camps, he didn't like outdoor sports, and above all things, he didn't like fishing. But you would have thought he was enjoying every minute of the day, particularly when we displayed our prize catch, a 43-pound catfish that must have been exceedingly revolting to the fastidious Mr. McKinley.

Some of our less understanding friends insisted that he should try his hand at fishing and, immaculate in frock coat and black tie, he manfully took a pole and ventured down to a rocky shelf along the river. There was a flat-bottomed boat pulled up on the shelf, half out of the water, and Mr. McKinley got into it in order to get his line farther out into the water. Strangely enough, he hooked a fish, but as he was trying to pull it in his weight slid the boat down the shelf and water began to come in over the stern. Slowly, the boat was sliding off the shelf and filling with water.

I was closest to him and I ran over to grab the sinking boat. The unhappy fisherman was already wet to the knees and rocking dangerously, but he turned with grave dignity and, holding his fishing pole aloft, staggered back to my end of the boat and then to the rock shelf. He never lost his good-humored composure, although I knew that he was thoroughly disgusted and must have felt like consigning us all to perdition as soon as he was alone in his sloshing shoes.

Instead, he thanked me and said jokingly, "You have saved my life, young man, and I shall always be indebted to you." Then as he tried to repair some of the damage to his clothes he kept up a steady stream of pleasant conversation, giving me sage advice on my future, and saying that perhaps one day he could help me with a job. Little did he know!

That was my first realization of the trials of a man who would be President, and I sometimes wonder what others would have done in the same circumstances. Teddy Roosevelt would have loved it, but I think Mr. Coolidge, for instance, would have set his lips in grim silence.

Mr. McKinley was probably the hand-shakingest President ever in the White House. There were normally three noontime receptions a week, at which long lines of visitors would gather to file past the Chief Executive. Mr. McKinley would take his place in the East Room, resplendent in frock coat and perhaps with a carnation pinned on his lapel, and the chief usher would open the doors. Sometimes the line of waiting visitors extended from the White House door out across the lawn and as far as the Treasury Building, a block away. It was a sight to strike horror into the heart of even a strong man, but Mr. McKinley took it in his stride.

Like all Presidents, he developed a technique of grasping a visitor's hand before the other fellow had time to clamp down, and thus, by holding the visitor's arm straight, he avoided having his own hand squeezed hard. Then he dragged the caller along as he shook hands, so that the line kept moving. Once he clasped 1200 hands in 19 minutes, or about one per second. That was some speed, but he never gave the impression that it was a heavy physical strain. Mr. McKinley was always in condition, because he was always shaking somebody's hand. Often he gave every sign of enjoying it, and I think he would have felt he was getting soft without a few hundred hands to shake every day.

These public affairs were only part of his heavy political schedule. The records of our office for one year showed that some 30,000 job-hunters dropped in at the White House, that an average of 20 Congressional callers were on the list daily, and that 70,000 persons visited the East Room. The President saw or shook hands with a large proportion of the visitors, and of course he held long conferences with some.

In a different classification were such influential regular callers as Senator Boies Penrose, the quiet, heavy-set Pennsylvania political boss, and Senator Mark Hanna of Ohio, who "owned" the President. The cartoonist always pictured Hanna as wearing clothes spangled with dollar marks, but not only was he the most conservative dresser in Congress, he was also one of the most unobtrusive visitors around the White House. Penrose was the only powerful political figure I knew who would write an endorsement of any job-hunter who happened to seek his help—so help me, anybody! We received hundreds of such letters from him, and we always treated them perfunctorily. We knew that they didn't mean anything and that he didn't expect us to pay any attention to them. If he was really interested in getting a job for someone, he would speak directly to the President—and he usually got action.

Two unusual women also were familiar figures to us—not because they had the run of the White House office, as did Penrose and Hanna, but because they were lobbyists. One was Dr. Mary Walter, a small, dried-up, and birdlike little woman who was a tireless worker for women's rights. She wore men's clothes and was looked upon publicly as a sort of freak, but she was a brilliant conversationalist and achieved a great deal by buttonholing legislators who came to the office. It was then against the law in many places for women to wear men's clothes, but Congress thought so highly of Dr. Walker that a special resolution was passed giving her the right to dress as she pleased anywhere in the United States or its territories. She always wore a dark coat, vest, shirt and tie, and trousers.

The other woman was Queen Lil, who wanted to succeed her brother on the throne of the Hawaiian Islands. She was fat, very dusky, and quite unlike the storybook picture of Hawaiian royalty, but she wore colorful and extravagant dresses, and for a while was one of the more spectacular sights of Washington. She came almost daily to the White House to ask whether the President had done anything about restoring her throne. He never had, and after some weeks she became discouraged and went back to her islands, where the President eventually installed a governor.

One of the reasons things ran smoothly at the White House was that there were men like George B. Cortelyou, who came in during the Cleveland administration, and who became secretary to Presidents McKinley and Theodore Roosevelt. He was perhaps the most competent and most thoughtful man I ever worked with, and he knew every detail of every job in the White House, from janitor to President. He was never too busy to help a befuddled young clerk, and I remember once walking in on him while he was in conference and asking him how I should describe a small pamphlet that had been sent to Mrs. McKinley and which I had been told to acknowledge. If he was annoyed, he gave no sign. Instead he gravely advised me to call it "a dainty publication," which is exactly what it was.

John Addison Porter, who was President McKinley's first secretary, had a violent temper, but he also indulged in outbursts of extreme friendliness. One of the thrills of my first days in the White House was an argument between Porter and Colonel (later General) Theodore Bingham, who became Police Commissioner of New York in 1906, but was then in charge of Buildings and Grounds. They frequently disagreed, and when they did the rest of the office quit work and gathered around just to see which could reach the highest peak of profanity and abuse. Both were good, but when they reached a point where they seemed ready to tear each other limb from limb, one would say, "Well, let's go to lunch," and they would walk off arm in arm.

We did a lot of work around the White House in those days, but we sometimes could coast along, too. I recall being kidded about the time old Uncle Warren Young, who was the roly-poly chief clerk, stopped by my desk and saw I was absent.

"Where's Ira?" he asked. Somebody said I was sick.

"Sick, eh?" Uncle Warren said, pointing to an item he had been reading on the sports page of his paper. "I see he bowled a good score in the tournament last night." (That was in the days when I was really rolling them!)

Everybody got a laugh out of it except Uncle Warren, who had to do my work, but we covered up for each other, and nobody complained about my one-day "illness."

The White House in McKinley's time was a poorly preserved and rat-infested old mansion that the President could neither get rid of nor get repaired. Representatives from out in the farming country were preponderant in Congress, and they thought the McKinleys were pretty goldarned lucky to have a big house like that free, especially when Congressmen had a time of it trying to find room and board in Washington for $2 a day. What did it matter if the kitchen needed a new coat of paint? Congress couldn't spare the money right then.

As a matter of fact, the mansion was not much changed from the time it had been rebuilt after being burned by the British. Even the grounds were almost the same, because every tree and bush was marked on the White House plans, and still is. Whenever a tree dies another of the same type is planted in its place.

You entered the front door (it was originally the back door) and found yourself in a lobby with a back wall made of colored glass, much like a church window, made by Tiffany. On the other side of the glass partition a corridor ran the length of the house from the East Room to the State Dining Room on the west. Off one side of the lobby was a little entry from which a narrow wooden stairway mounted to the second floor, making two turns on the way. After the second turn you came to a landing and a door opening into a wide corridor lined with chairs and a table or two. This was a sort of lobby where callers waited their turn.

The Lincoln Room served as a private office for the President, but he had another larger office next door and, adjoining that, a corner office for his secretary. When I first went to the White House as a rather aimless young man just out of college, I worked in the office of Secretary Porter for a few months. I never felt much awe of famous people, but I was interested in the parade of dignitaries, and I probably took on some inflated ideas about my own importance now that I was on the White House staff. Even though I was appointed through political pull and Porter merely stuck me at a desk until he could find a job for me, I thought that it wasn't just anybody who could step into such historic surroundings.

That's why I remember so clearly "the man who let him out." He came into the office after I had been there twiddling my thumbs for a few days and approached me gravely, a big man with a grizzled beard, but grown old and shrunken into his clothes. He looked at me with watery eyes, looked out the window at the swamps leading down to the Potomac, and introduced himself as Pop Pendel.

"I'm the man who let him out," he explained in a quiet voice.

"How's that?" I asked.

"The way it was that night," he said, "was that he come down to the front door where the others was waiting for him. I remember it clear. The carriage was waiting and ready to take them to the theater where some famous lady was performing in a stage show. A famous actress. . . . Well, they was all ready to go and they come over to the door where I was standing, because I was an usher then just like I am now. He was walking tall and straight and he smiled pleasant-like at me and I opened the door for him to go down to Ford's Theatre. I'm the man who let him out."

He stared out the window again and I thought he must be remembering that dreadful night and the shot fired at Ford's Theatre and the infamy of John Wilkes Booth, but instead he pointed a long finger at the window.

"I used to see him lots of times during the war standing right where you are with the saddest look on his face," he said. "He would stand here at night and look out this window and he could see the campfires across the river and nobody knew just how close the rebels were or whether they were getting ready for an attack on Washington. He would stand here looking until late at night sometimes."

Pop Pendel turned around and started out, but halfway to the door he said: "I was in the Army before I was an usher here." Then he went on his way. I heard him tell the story many times, and he was always "the man who let him out."

When Porter later put me in charge of the President's mail, I was moved across the hall, where the staff worked. There was one large room for the assistant secretary and a half-dozen clerks. Then there was another narrow room at the northeast corner. In it were a telegraph operator, a three-foot-high boxlike contraption with a dial that served as a house telephone and my desk. Oh yes, there was also a partitioned-off corner that concealed the office toilet.

It was sometimes a little difficult under these conditions for me to maintain the feeling of dignity that I had fostered when I sat where Lincoln had looked out the window, but at least everybody in the offices came around every so often, and usually stopped for a chat. Everybody except the President, who took advantage of the plumbing facilities in his living quarters at the other end of the house.

There was an elevator in the White House, but it operated on water pressure from a tank on the roof, and usually the pressure was low and the elevator declined to run. The only time it ever seemed likely that we would get Congressional approval for White House repairs was when some stout Senator or Representative would call on the President and have to puff up the winding stairs. Many of them complained bitterly, and couldn't understand why the McKinleys didn't keep the machinery in good shape.

Mr. McKinley would listen gravely to their complaints and nod his head, but later when I said something to him about the problem, he merely smiled.

"Let them complain," he remarked with a good deal of feeling. "It's too easy for them to get up here the way it is."

The presidential mail was not heavy in comparison with today's but, as I have said, it ran about 100 letters a day and in times of crisis mounted to 1000 or more, most of them from citizens who wanted Mr. McKinley either to get into war with Spain in a hurry or to stay out of war with Spain. The prowar writers bitterly denounced the President as a coward and a pussyfooter. He took these attacks calmly, and spent more time than necessary explaining that it was his duty to encourage every possibility of a peaceful settlement.

It is difficult to draw a line, but these letters and telegrams were one of the early forms of organized propaganda mail that eventually grew to a huge volume. I didn't take much stock in obviously inspired letters at that time, and in later years I was even less impressed, but I knew some Presidents who were influenced by the erroneous belief that they were listening to the voice of the people. My own idea was that if a man couldn't make up his own mind after he knew the facts, he didn't have any business being President.

Mr. McKinley was scrupulous about making members of his family pull their own weight, and he refused a commission to his nephew during the war, but he was less rigid in regard to his friends. I recall one instance in which a hot-tempered young journalist got in a rather sensational jam that was almost the reverse of the famous Patton slapping incident of World War II.

Sylvester Scoville, son of a president of Wooster University, which I had attended, became a newspaper correspondent in Cuba during the war and was dashing around Santiago when the Spanish forces capitulated. He went to the headquarters of General William Shafter to get a statement about the surrender. Shafter was one of those hardheaded old soldiers who didn't understand much about the press, and he was not of a mind to give out any information.

The impetuous young reporter argued with him without success and, in a flash of temper, slapped Shafter across the face and stalked out. The General fumed and fussed, but in those days there were no definite rules for dealing with correspondents, and all he could do was ship Scoville back to Washington without delay. There was a lot of speculation as to what would happen to him, and for several days some very influential political figures from Ohio wandered into the White House to ask the President to go easy.

One day Scoville himself came by. He was a merry and dashing young man in a wrinkled suit, and I felt rather sympathetic toward him, but the President declined to receive him. I told him I had attended Wooster University and invited him out for a drink, which he seemed to need at that point. We went around to a famous but exclusive old bar that was reached only by going through a dusty storeroom where whisky cases were stacked high along the walls. Scoville explained that he was sorry about the slapping incident, and had merely wanted to apologize to the President. We talked it over and decided that they couldn't do much other than charge him with disorderly conduct, and after a few drinks, we went out and had a fine dinner. Eventually, Mr.

McKinley chose to ignore the whole affair and let it die out without taking any action.

The death of Mr. McKinley at the hands of a crazed assassin was a terrible blow to the White House staff. We spent days and nights waiting beside the telegraph instrument for word from his bedside in Buffalo, sending out for food and sleeping in chairs in the office. We almost lynched a callous young reporter who wandered in late one evening and remarked that he was tired of waiting for the end and wished the President would "get it over with."

When it was all over, we felt that things would never be the same again, and we looked forward with extreme uneasiness to the administration of Theodore Roosevelt. We feared we would be housed with a sort of wild-eyed man who might fire us at once or dispatch us without warning on a big-game hunting expedition in Tibet.

But the famous T.R. came in like a lamb, and in time we recovered the feeling that we were all one big family—at times a boisterous and squabbling family, but never separated by any severe formality or unnecessary dignity as far as the President was concerned. Occasionally, we would have given a good deal for a greater degree of separation from the rest of the family, but at least there was something doing all the time.

## CHAPTER FOUR

As I look back on my experiences in Washington it seems to me that one of the most pleasantly exciting periods was the era of the first Roosevelts in the White House. The times generally were unforgettable because of such natural and historical phenomena as honeymoons at Niagara Falls, shirt-waists, and high hair-dos, muckracking, the American debut of Caruso, and the inventive daring of Langley, whose airplane didn't fly, and the Wright brothers, whose airplane did.

In particular the times were exciting around the White House, too, because you never knew what on earth might turn up in the next mail delivery, although you could be fairly certain that it would be something surprising. The President's love of hunting, especially big-game hunting, and other sports prompted persons all over the world to send him trophies and, frequently, live animals. We had plenty of eagles, dogs, lizards, and even the two beautiful Nubian lions from Africa already mentioned, all of which would have made a fine start on a private zoo in the mail room. It soon became apparent, however, that things were going to be lively enough without a zoo at 1600 Pennsylvania Avenue.

Many letters for T.R. arrived with a drawing or a cartoon of him on the envelope, or sometimes with only a toothy grin and a large pair of pince-nez spectacles as the only address. The Post Office knew where to deliver such letters even if the envelope had nothing on it but a drawing of a "big stick."

But for my money the period was most exciting because, in my opinion, T.R. was about twenty years ahead of his time. And I say that grudgingly, because his working pace certainly interfered with my fishing expeditions and my bowling score was a disgrace for lack of practice.

When T.R. arrived at the White House, he asked us to carry on as we had been doing. That, however, was a mere figure of speech, because the pace was immediately stepped up. He usually got to his desk at 9 A.M., and expected everything to go into high gear at once. That meant I had to get to work at least an hour earlier in order to have everything ready. Then the whirlwind would begin.

Mr. Roosevelt wrote to experts everywhere on such subjects as conservation and antitrust legislation, and he gathered an amazing file of information, ideas, theories, and practical suggestions for use in forming his own opinions. No suggestion was too advanced or too trivial for his attention. No subject was too esoteric for him; he could and would discuss almost anything with anybody and at least give the impression that he was well informed in the field. Often he was.

We compiled a record of all of his correspondence, both before and after becoming President, and he drew on it freely in preparation of his speeches. The overtime efforts of the whole staff were needed to keep up with him when he was preparing a speech. He dictated to Rudolph Forster, the executive clerk, and the rest of us brought him records or transcribed Forster's shorthand notes in relays.

His daily routine was almost as hectic, but with certain regular breaks. One was when he went to the Cabinet Room to be shaved by John Mays, a colored usher who was still at the White House when I retired in 1948. Mays would lather the President's face and get to work, but something always interrupted him. Sometimes a caller would arrive and the secretary would inform Mr. Roosevelt, who often had him brought into the Cabinet Room to talk while he was still being barbered. At other times I would open an important letter and take it to him at once and he would hold it out at arm's length, squinting his eyes and puffing lather as he read. If it was of immediate importance, he would call a secretary and tell him what to say in reply. Mays kept right on at his job all the time with inimitable patience and skill.

Another regular event of the day was T.R.'s exercise. It was almost always of a violent nature, even when he just went for a walk. He would often walk on a rainy day, and he loved to wade across streams, tear through underbrush, and roam over a few hills. The Secret Service men who had to follow wherever he went would come back muddy and in wild disarray, and frequently with a bitter and beaten look in their eyes.

On other days, the President played tennis, went horseback riding, boxed with his trainer, Sixsmith, or maybe with Mike

Donovan when Mike was in town. He also tried jujitsu at one point, taking lessons from an expert from Japan.

The President's love of sports and big-game hunting was an interesting and, to me, an often amusing story. I've always liked sports myself. I pitched some pretty good baseball in my day, I could hit a hard tennis ball, and I had killed a score of deer before I was fifteen years old. So I always watched and listened when the President played or talked sports.

He had been a sickly child, what he described as "pigeon-breasted and asthmatic." But he had plenty of determination and boundless courage, and through the years he built himself into a rugged hiker, rider, and mountain-climber. His eyes were always weak, however, and one of them was damaged further as the result of a clumsy encounter during one of his White House boxing matches. I never heard it admitted, but it seemed to me that he had virtually lost the sight of that eye.

Many of his tennis matches were played just outside a window of our office, and I often watched him in action. His approach to the game was as energetic as Suzanne Lenglen's, but without the same results. He jumped up and down continually when he was playing the net, but when the ball came his way he was strictly a "pusher" who shoved it in the general direction of the net. Since he also sometimes had trouble in gauging distances, and since he usually played with members of his family who had no respect for his high office, the President never made any remarkable impression as a racket-wielder. He did, however, get plenty of exercise, and his happy cry of "Bully shot!" or "Bully for you!" was the best I ever heard on a tennis court.

I never got a chance to ask the Japanese expert how the President did at jujitsu, but at any rate he talked it expertly, although less often than he talked of big-game hunting. On one of his vacations he made a hunting trip in search of small black bears that were found in the cane brakes of Mississippi. There was a lot in the newspapers about Mr. Roosevelt's prowess as a hunter, some of it serious and some amusing, and it was at that time that Clifford Berryman, the cartoonist for the *Washington Star,* created the famous Teddy bear. There was a strange story in some of the newspapers about the President's refusing to shoot a small bear that had been brought into camp by a woodsman. Berryman drew a cartoon of T.R., gun in hand and Rough Rider hat cocked on his head, motioning away a wistful, frightened, wonderful little black bear. The title was "Drawing the Line." The little animal, as the Teddy bear, became so popular that Berryman frequently worked it into his cartoons in succeeding years.

This was the beginning of the Teddy-bear craze that spread everywhere. At first the manufacturers made them principally for adults, but they were so loved by children that they still remain a big seller on the toy market. The toymakers later tried various other animals, but never found one comparable to the Teddy bear. It was a great publicity stunt for Mr. Roosevelt, and he loved it.

I took a particular interest in the President's hunting exploits in general because I was always curious about how good a shot he was, and I liked the Teddy-bear mania in general because it reminded me of a childhood experience of mine in the California mountains near Santa Ynez, when my father was first taking us to that ranch he had bought high up in the Cachuma Valley. I was nine years old, and I wore a tight-fitting little knitted suit that had been bought in East Liverpool, Ohio, where knitted suits were the rage that year among the mamas of boys under ten. Among *boys* under ten they were a pain in the neck.

I had a .22 rifle that my father had foolishly given me, and I didn't ask anybody's permission when I got up before breakfast and left our overnight camp to hunt for bears. I had never fired the rifle, and I was still trying to figure out how it worked when I met a Mexican about two hundred yards from our camp. He was a lean, brown-faced fellow in faded overalls, and when I first saw him he was smiling at me as if he had never seen anything so odd in the mountains. I scowled fiercely to cover up my embarrassment. He immediately became serious and asked where I was going. I replied tersely that I was going hunting for bear.

"Bear?" he repeated, still looking at my tight city suit and shaking his head. "Better not. Bears not like to be shot at."

I wasn't going to be discouraged by any such nonsense as that, and I still didn't like the smile that flickered around the corners of his mouth. But I did weaken when he said that the bears all went far up to the mountaintop in the daytime. Anyway, I could smell the bacon frying back at the camp by then, and I accepted his suggestion that we walk back and get some breakfast. He ate several helpings of bacon as he talked over with Mother the dangers of nine-year-olds hunting bears, but mostly he just kept looking at my knitted suit and shaking his head in melancholy amusement.

He was right. The suit didn't last long in the mountains, but I lasted quite a while, including a number of periods when I hunted for days by myself and if I didn't kill anything I didn't eat. As I remember it, I always ate. I suppose T.R. could have killed his own food, too, but I was always puzzled by the fact that a man with such poor eyesight could be such a famous hunter. Of course, things are made somewhat simpler by guides and expert marksmen and beaters when the hunter is also the President of the United States. And Mr. Roosevelt made up in enthusiasm and bounce for anything that he may have been lacking.

The President not only played games to the limit but he was a man of strong opinions (outside his own household), and he thought everyone else ought to take his viewpoint about sports. He ordered all mounted Army officers at Fort Myer to get their spurs off their desk and go on regular riding expeditions to show they could still do it. Some of these rides were thirty miles, and Mr. Roosevelt went along to be sure they didn't take any short cuts.

On one occasion a couple of small newsboys got in a rumpus and exchanged a few blows on a street corner outside our office. They were likable kids, and we persuaded them to put on boxing gloves in the White House basement to settle their quarrel. They did, and word of the encounter got to Mr. Roosevelt. He had them brought into his office to fight it out. With such an audience, the kids slugged each other's brains out for as long as they could stand on their feet, and the President cheered them on.

Every so often one or more of T.R.'s famous Rough Riders

would turn up at the White House, some of them in a restless search for the excitement they had known during the war and others in the uncertain hope of speaking again to the man who had been their Colonel at San Juan Hill. Their reputation was one of the President's political assets, and he always managed to make them welcome. Occasionally they would be entertained far beyond their greatest expectations at the White House, where T.R. always liked to have guests when he sat down at the table even if he had to invite whatever caller happened to be in the office at the time.

The Rough Riders were a strange assortment of Indians, cowboys, frontiersmen, and college graduates, and some of the less stable ones became familiar characters around Washington. I remember one in picturesque uniform who stayed at the old Ebbitt House, where he was usually surrounded by a group of idlers. After a few hours of sitting around the lobby and spinning yarns he moved out to sit on the curbstone. His listeners followed, and one of them asked why he had left the lobby.

"Them danged chairs is too soft for me," he answered.

Another not-so-soft visitor was Eli Smith, who traveled from Nome, Alaska, with a sledge and six dogs to call on Mr. Roosevelt. It took him about a year to make the trip overland—except for a short boat journey—and he was supposed to have won a bet of $10,000. The President welcomed him and gave him a certificate showing the date of his arrival.

In the same year, 1907, we welcomed Ezra Meeker, who drove an ox team and covered wagon from Tacoma, Washington. It took him two years. The President had a long talk with the grizzled but spry old man.

In addition to such official visitors, the White House was a lively place because of the activities of the Roosevelt children and their friends. At home, Mrs. Roosevelt was the dominant member of that family, and she believed that children ought to be allowed to express themselves and self-develop their own personalities. There was so much self-expression and so much personality around the place that at times it seemed likely Congress would be forced to settle the old quarrel over building a new White House because the old one was going to be torn apart.

The boys—Kermit, Archie, Teddy, and Quentin—were encouraged to be athletic, and when several of them engaged in a rousing game of cowboy and Indian they regarded not only the living quarters but the halls and offices as the wide open range. They went through like a small cyclone, or perhaps a charge up San Juan Hill. They played soldier with the tops of garbage cans for shields and wooden sticks for swords, and their favorite point of attack was likely to be the shins of a busy clerk or stenographer. They were dead shots with a beanshooter, and their most frequent target was the shining bald head of one of the telegraph operators. On occasion, outsiders suffered, too, as when Kermit hid behind some bushes and threw mud on passing carriages.

I suppose it is only logical to say that the staff regarded them as spoiled brats, but their mother seldom reprimanded them, and never allowed them to be punished, because it might retard the natural development of their personalities.

Sometimes this built up in the staff a keen desire to indulge in a little self-expression of our own.

One Sunday Ethel Roosevelt, who was then about twelve years old, came into the offices swinging an inch-thick stick that had been cut off a tree and trimmed. She walked up to Jim Smithers, the chief telegrapher and telephone operator, who was reading a newspaper and had his feet up on the desk.

"Smithers," she said, "put up the tennis net for me."

He didn't care much for the way she said it and paid no attention.

"Did you hear me?" she demanded.

Smithers said he was not permitted to leave his post.

"So you refuse?"

Ethel raised the stick—it had rough little knobs on it where the branches had been trimmed—and whammed Smithers on the shins with all her strength, cutting his leg. Smithers expressed *his* personality by grabbing her and turning her across his lap, face down, and giving her a few lusty whacks with his hand on the most available spot. She howled, and just then Smithers looked up and saw T.R. standing in the doorway watching. The President walked over and grabbed Ethel by the shoulder and put her out the door.

"Didn't I tell you," he said, "never to come in these offices?"

He never said a word to Smithers, who called me into his office to see the cut. Where a knob on the stick had dug into his shin, a scar always remained.

Once when Archie was sick, his brothers decided that something should be done to cheer him up. The best idea they could generate was that he would like to see his Shetland pony. The White House stables were then about halfway down to the Potomac, and the boys were in the habit of riding their spotted pony up to the yard, so nobody paid any attention when they arrived on this occasion. They led the pony in through the basement door and brought the elevator down to that level. The docile beast entered with no difficulties, but, as I remember the incident, the elevator stuck between floors on the way up to Archie's room. It took the combined efforts of the Secret Service men and the ushers to get them down and out again, and I, for one, always rather regretted their failure. It was a good brotherly sentiment.

Almost everybody around the White House liked animals in that period. The President had a little bulldog he was fond of, but it had an overdeveloped sense of its own importance. On one occasion it took a dislike to Ambassador Jusserand of France, a frequent guest, and attacked him as he was leaving the grounds. The newspapers reported that the dog had chased the Ambassador up a tree, but I'm not sure that it did more than tear one leg of his trousers—which was insult enough, because Jusserand was a dapper little Frenchman with a trim Vandyke beard.

Anyway, the dog became something of a celebrity, and a short time later one of the reporters wrote a story about how it had been disgracefully licked by a stray cur that wandered into the grounds. After reading the story, a man out in Ohio sent T.R. a letter saying that he had shipped him a dog that "can lick any dog in the world." The animal arrived three days later, and I opened the box and let him out. He immediately ran around the office sprinkling every desk and the legs of most of the staff. I shoved him quickly out a window and then went out and put a rope around his neck. He was a strange-looking creature, with the long head of a bull terrier, the shoulders of a bulldog, a short body, powerful legs, and a short tail.

"Let's see him," the President said when I told him of the gift. He gave the dog a long puzzled look, and asked: "What'll we do with him?"

Jim Smithers, the chief telegrapher, asked for him and got him. In collaboration with Bob Anderson, a tall, red-headed Negro messenger, the dog was matched in a number of dog fights with sizable betting. The Ohio dog didn't fool around about his fighting. He would feint the other dog out of position, dive in, and clamp his teeth into the back of his foe's neck and, with a mighty tug, hurl him over his shoulder. The other dog was nearly always dead when he hit the ground.

Of all the Roosevelt children, I felt that Quentin, who lost his life as an aviator in World War I, was the most likable as a child. He was a chubby little boy at that time, and he collected autographs. I saved many signatures, including those of foreign dignitaries, for him, until he finally decided to give up the hobby. When he did give it up he was at Oyster Bay, and he sent me his collector's book with a little note saying that he was tired of it but he thought I might want to carry on.

Alice was, of course, the most talked-about of the children. But she was older and we didn't see much of her around the executive office. She and the Countess Cassini spent a great deal of time shocking Washington society by smoking and going unchaperoned. I must say she was a handsome figure when she was dressed up in the smart clothes of that day, which, as I remember, included a dashing broad-brimmed hat tipped over one eye. Her wedding to Nicholas Longworth was a newspaper sensation for days, and gifts, including some rare snakes and a hogshead of popcorn, poured into the White House from all over the United States and from many foreign countries.

"Princess" Alice, as she was called, didn't get along especially well with Mrs. Roosevelt, who was her step-mother. My sympathies were on Alice's side. One reason was that I felt that Mrs. Roosevelt had a rather overbearing attitude toward the staff in general and, as a result of one incident, toward me in particular.

I played baseball in college and have always kept up with the game. Several of us had a habit of playing catch on the White House lawn during the luncheon hour in the McKinley administration, and with the full approval of Mr. McKinley. The first time we did it after T.R. came in, Mrs. Roosevelt looked out the window and was shocked to see young men with their coats off disporting themselves on "her" lawn. Mrs. Roosevelt called the office and told off Rudolph Forster, the executive clerk, who assured her that it would not happen again. She was not satisfied, however, and she telegraphed to the President, who at the time was out in Yellowstone National Park. T.R. replied that a reprimand was being dispatched, but that still wasn't enough. Mrs.

Roosevelt felt that we ought to be deprived of our annual leave. The President eventually agreed with her and issued the order, but when the time came it was not enforced. We didn't ever feel that T.R., in view of his own love of athletics, took the offense very seriously.

Throughout his administration Mr. Roosevelt showed himself to be a keen student of publicity and an able hand at employing it to achieve his ends. He also enjoyed coining new phrases and words, of which "Tread softly and carry a big stick" was the most successful. Another that he used many times was "nature fakirs," a term he aimed at journalist-adventurers who wrote about impossible experiences with wild animals or of incredible journeys in distant lands.

It was in the Roosevelt administration that the idea of press conferences began to emerge, particularly after T.R. had the executive-office wing added to the White House. But even before the offices were moved from the second floor he would occasionally talk to the reporters who were waiting in our office for news or to buttonhole callers. This custom did not start off with any appreciation of the importance that was to be attained by modern White House press conferences, but T.R. soon realized the value of personally giving the news to all the reporters at the same time, and he made good use of the system to get his viewpoint across to the public.

He would wait until there was some announcement to hand out in typewritten form and then he would step into the corridor and get the reporters together, explaining to them his ideas on the subject. It was nothing like the give-

and-take of today's press conferences. The President was a man who didn't appreciate interruptions, and who sometimes seemed to use his high position to talk down anyone who disagreed with him. There were never any embarrassing questions asked by reporters in those days.

There were no telephones for reporters, either, and whenever news broke at the White House there would be a mad scramble down the twisting stairway to the ground floor, where the President's statement would be handed to waiting bicycle messengers, who pedaled off furiously to the newspaper offices.

T.R. was impatient with many of the stereotyped methods of government operation, and it was his custom to order quick and drastic changes when they came to his attention. During the period when he was Civil Service Commissioner he came across the examination that was standard for persons seeking jobs as mounted inspectors along the Rio Grande River. The questions covered history, rhetoric, and mathematics, and Mr. Roosevelt disgustedly tore it up and wrote a new set of questions himself. His questions covered such problems as how to break a wild horse and how to handle a cow pony that had been turned loose to graze for six months.

"You don't need to know algebra or the latitude of Zanzibar for that job," he barked. "I'm only sorry I can't add to the test a requirement that each applicant lasso, throw, and tie a steer in twenty seconds."

He also was one of the foremost advocates of simplified spelling, using such words as *nite, thot, tho,* and *thru* in his letters. Lots of people wrote in to encourage his spelling campaign, but there were plenty of complaints, too.

We developed a great fondness for Mr. Roosevelt, despite the extra work he piled on the staff, because he was always fair and courteous and he worked even harder than we did. When he left the White House it was typical that he should call us together and make a little speech. It was always interesting to hear him speak, because he had a peculiar style that was marked by long pauses between sentences or in the middle of a sentence, after which he would rattle off a string of staccato words like a burst from a machine gun. Frequently they were surprising words, too.

"Gentlemen," he said, when we had assembled, "I want to express my earnest appreciation of the services that you have rendered. . . ." A long pause while he gave us a friendly big-tooth smile. "I have often thought you would have been warranted in getting up a conspiracy to assassinate me because of the way I have worked you!" Another pause. "I wouldn't have blamed you at all. Now, I do not wish to leave without having the pleasure of shaking hands with each of you individually."

We were sorry to see him go, although we were not exactly depressed by the departure of the rest of the family—particularly the kids. But we didn't realize that with T.R. went an atmosphere that would never be wholly recaptured around the White House. The feeling that we were one big family was soon to end. We were getting too big—almost too big for our britches.

We didn't know that, however, when we first met Mr. Taft.

We didn't know how much Mr. Taft enjoyed dancing and social affairs, even though his great weight made his feet hurt on such occasions. We didn't know about his love of food, or how irritated he could become when forced to diet. We were ignorant of a lot of things when the Tafts moved in. Why, we didn't even know that it was supposed to be Mrs. Taft who really liked the idea of living in the White House and who was largely responsible for her husband's succession to T.R.

## CHAPTER FIVE

EVERY MAN HAS HIS SMALL TROUBLES, EVEN IF HE HAPPENS to be President of the United States. Or should I say especially *if* he is President of the United States?

I don't hesitate about saying it, because of the nine Presidents I've seen in action at the White House all have had their personal woes, just as I've had mine. Now my trouble is that I like to bet on the race horses. When it comes to picking a winner in the fifth race at Havre de Grace, I'd rather be right than President. It's been a lot of fun, but at times it has meant a lot of trouble, too. Just like being President.

The troubles of William Howard Taft, however, were not the usual presidential woes that became familiar to me. One of Mr. Taft's troubles was food. He loved it, and the more food he could get, the more he loved it. The rub was that after he moved into the White House, his doctor and Mrs. Taft were constantly on the alert to enforce a diet that would get rid of some of his surplus poundage. Mrs. Taft might reasonably be described as a strong-minded woman. She took dieting seriously—for the President—and this led to a lot of talk that in a less famous household might have been called nagging.

The President dieted, all right, but not when he could escape supervision. I remember once when I accompanied him on a journey to Ohio. When we got on the train, leaving the doctor and Mrs. Taft behind, the President began to perk up. He also apparently began to think about food, although it was then ten o'clock in the evening. Wilbur Hinman, a stenographer, and I were in the observation section of Mr. Taft's special car going through telegrams and letters when the President appeared at the door of his sitting room. A pleasant smile turned the corners of his mouth. I took one look and knew what was on his mind.

"Anybody seen the conductor?" he asked.

The conductor came a-running.

"The dining car . . ." Mr. Taft began shyly. "Could we get a snack?"

The conductor looked surprised. "Why, Mr. President, there isn't any dining car on this train."

The President's sun-tanned face turned pink, with perhaps a few splashes of purple. His normally prominent eyes seemed to bulge.

"Norton!" he called in a cold voice. "Mr. Norton!"

Charles D. Norton, a tall, good-looking, and well-dressed man, appeared from the next compartment. He was Mr. Taft's secretary, and he probably had been given special instructions by Mrs. Taft in regard to the President's diet on the trip.

"Mr. Norton," the President said, "there is no diner on this train."

Norton agreed that there was no diner. He reminded Mr. Taft that they had had dinner at the White House, and assured him that they would not go without breakfast. He recalled that the President's doctor had warned him about eating between meals. The President brushed him aside, turning back to the conductor.

"What's the next stop, dammit?" he asked. "The next stop where there's a diner?"

The conductor believed that would be Harrisburg. Mr. Taft glared at Norton and addressed the conductor:

"I am President of the United States, and I want a diner attached to this train at Harrisburg. I want it well stocked with food, including filet mignon. You see that we get a diner." He silenced the secretary's protests with a roar. "What's the use of being President," he demanded, "if you can't have a train with a diner on it?"

Norton gave up. The diner was attached at Harrisburg in the middle of the night, and the President had the newspapermen advised that it was open to them. He sat in his own car for a long time, partaking of refreshments. He seemed to be in high good humor. Personally, I applauded him for his humanness in kicking over the traces when he had the opportunity.

The problem of food harassed Mr. Taft throughout his administration, and I always felt that it added considerably to his unhappiness with the high office he occupied. But it was only one of his woes. He could have doubled Harry

Truman in spades when the Missourian once remarked that he hadn't ever wanted to be President.

Even inaugural day was a bad one for Mr. Taft. A heavy rain that turned to sticky wet snow swept over Washington and filled the streets with slush. A number of stands for spectators had been built in front of the Treasury, the State Department, and the White House, but only the White House seats were covered. The storm stopped in the morning, but conditions were so bad that few spectators wanted to sit in the uncovered stands, and there was frantic bidding for protected places in front of the White House.

Each member of the staff had been given four seats in the covered stands, and I know that one clerk turned a neat profit by calling at the expensive hotels until he found a wealthy New York woman who paid $250 for his tickets. Many persons who had come to Washington especially for the inauguration did not even leave their hotels because of the weather. The afternoon before the ceremonies, a man bundled up in a huge fur coat drove his automobile up close to the presidential stands and climbed up on the seat of the car to wave a handful of currency at several of us who were standing in the White House driveway.

"I'll pay a thousand dollars for four seats in these stands," he shouted.

I was tempted, but my knowledge of the Secret Service objections to unidentified persons near the President convinced me that I should hold onto my tickets.

With the inauguration over, Mr. Taft took comparatively little interest in the staff except to make it clear that the fewer matters there were requiring his personal attention, the better he would like it. He didn't read letters if he could avoid it, and only the most important ones ever reached him. Even these were briefed so he could get through them quickly. I do not mean that Mr. Taft neglected the duties of his office, but his great interest was in the law courts (where he served so brilliantly) and he was not attracted to many of the routine details of life in the White House. It was also a relatively quiet period in history, and his inclination was to let uninteresting matters slide along. In many cases this gave the impression that he was discourteous, if I may state the facts mildly.

There were times when the waiting room and the office of his secretary—Fred Carpenter was the first one—would become overcrowded with visitors while the President prolonged a conversation with some friend whom he particularly enjoyed. Carpenter would fuss and fret and tender apologies to important but stranded callers, and occasionally he would appear at the door of Mr. Taft's office to remind him that visitors with definite appointments were waiting. Often he was ignored.

Naturally, many callers became incensed, and a considerable number of them were important political figures in their own localities. Some men who had traveled a long distance to see the President would be kept waiting for several days. Frequently they went home in disgust without ever getting into Mr. Taft's office.

Politicians were not the only ones kept waiting outside Mr. Taft's door. I recall one occasion when a group from the Metropolitan Opera was appearing in Washington and it was arranged for them to visit the President. They were an unusual group in those days, predominantly foreigners and predominantly long on temperament and short on funds. The male members of the group wore rather shiny blue suits and appeared to have gone too long without a haircut. The women were perhaps better dressed, but they blended into a nondescript off-stage picture as they took chairs in the lobby of the executive office to await Mr. Taft's pleasure.

They waited quite a while, patiently and with a quiet acceptance of delay that contrasted with the irritability of most American callers, who expected punctuality even from the head of the state. I noticed in particular one placid woman with a broad, pleasant face. There was something very familiar and very warm about her, but I couldn't seem to get it straight in my mind.

After half an hour of waiting there was a flurry at the main door, where a handsome limousine with a liveried chauffeur had drawn up. Then in swept Mary Garden, glistening with jewels, draped in furs and satin and looking like a million dollars. Escorted by Senator Frelinghuysen, she walked straight to the President's office and the door closed behind her—leaving the rest of the Opera group sitting just where they were. Miss Garden reappeared and departed in another sunburst of glamour about thirty minutes later and then the others were shown into Mr. Taft's office to shake hands.

When they came out, I again noticed the pleasant, broad-browed woman and I nudged one of the clerks as she passed.

"She looks familiar," I said. "Who is she?"

He smiled cynically. "Oh, nobody much," he said with

broad sarcasm. "Just the greatest singer alive—Madame Schumann-Heink. No glamour."

Now I do not presume to suggest that these incidents were the result of intentional rudeness on the part of the President. But it was obvious on various occasions that, for one reason or another, Mr. Taft passed up opportunities to make friends and influence people, particularly those on the White House staff. It had been customary, for instance, for the President to give each of the White House employees a Christmas gift. Mr. McKinley gave each member of the staff a photograph or a book. Theodore Roosevelt gave each clerk a $5 gold piece, and each policeman and messenger got a turkey.

When this custom was brought to Mr. Taft's attention at the proper time, he remarked: "I don't see why I should have to give them anything." And he didn't, so far as the clerical staff was concerned. And after all, why should he?

The President enjoyed playing golf, and on a sunny afternoon he might break all appointments on short notice and take off for the links with several friends. If this meant putting off the call of some political bigwig or delaying the date on which he received an ambassador, it did not appear to bother the President unduly. Nor did it impress him that the staff was often forced to sit idly awaiting his return from the golf links or from a late afternoon automobile ride in order to wind up the business of the day and get home, perhaps at 9 P.M., to a cold dinner.

These conditions were particularly acute during the first part of Mr. Taft's administration. Eventually, the President's political advisers began to worry about the unfavorable reaction that had set in among disgruntled politicians. Some of them blamed Carpenter, a mild but pleasant man whom Mr. Taft had brought to the White House when he was inaugurated. I never felt that Carpenter was particularly at fault, except that he always wanted to please the President and thus was ineffective in trying to correct the situation that had arisen.

In any even, the advisers decided that a new secretary was essential, and they wanted a "live wire" who could put the pieces together again and bring some order into the White House routine. They decided their man was Charles D. Norton, an up-and-coming man who was then Assistant Secretary of the Treasury. I think all of us were ready to welcome any change, believing it could only be for the better, but we didn't know what was in store for us.

Norton had a reputation for doing three things at once, and he also had the energy and the boldness to try to live up to that reputation, sometimes with strange results. He was the first modern efficiency expert I had ever seen in action, and I'm afraid that my reaction was to wish for a return to the catch-as-catch-can days of the gay nineties. His first move was to advise us that he wanted men with brains and a college background on the staff. He didn't inquire whether any of us had either, but it was clear that there was to be a housecleaning.

Now I have nothing against efficiency or bustle or brains, but I don't like to overdo any of them, and I feel that a fellow's morale may be improved by an occasional week-end fishing trip down the Potomac. Under Norton's supervision it was clear that I wasn't going to be called upon to do much relaxing. My working hours increased from 7:30 in the morning to 6 in the evening, and after dinner from 9 to midnight. In winter I never saw my wife or baby in daylight except on Sunday, when I only worked from 9:30 A.M. to 3 P.M. In order to speed things up, Norton presented me with ten little rubber stamps that were to be used for letters which I forwarded to the various departments. The dates had to be changed each day with a pair of tweezers, and it was so much quicker to write the name of the department on each letter that I never used them.

Norton took an immediate dislike to Wendell Mischler, who was Mr. Taft's personal stenographer. He dictated Mischler's resignation to Mischler, told him to "sign it and give it to me."

Mischler said he would do nothing of the sort. He walked out, and for the next two weeks he tried to get to see the President. Several times he went to the front door of the White House after Mr. Taft left his office, but Norton had apparently given orders for him to be refused admittance even though he was a personal friend of Mrs. Taft.

Finally, A. I. Vorhys, Republican national committeeman from Ohio, came to see the President and Mischler told him his story.

"Come with me," Vorhys said, adding a few choice bits of profanity. Norton tried to stop them when they got to the door of the President's office, but Vorhys shoved him aside and they walked in. Vorhys explained the situation.

"Is this your wish, Mr. President?" he asked.

Mr. Taft looked at him in surprise and replied: "Why, Mischler is the last man I would want to see go."

Needless to say, this sort of thing did not make Norton

popular in the office. Since I read all his mail, it would have been almost impossible for me not to have known his business pretty thoroughly, especially his financial affairs, and it wasn't difficult either to learn of long-distance conversations through the switchboard operators. He had been associated with a large life insurance company before coming to the White House, and he was still receiving large sums in commissions from past sales. He was interested in a South American bond issue in which some powerful financiers were lending a hand. When a man is unpopular with his office force, he is usually watched, but there was nothing unethical in Mr. Norton's operations. It is well known that many prominent persons come into government service at a small salary because they are considered valuable material for the particular job, and they continue their outside interests with full official approval.

While the South American negotiations were in progress, Norton warned all of us, "This is strictly confidential, and if any word of it gets out I will find out who did it and fire the guilty person." Since we had been handling confidential matters for years without any leaks, we naturally resented this attitude, and Arthur Leonard, one of the office correspondents, told Norton, "I don't know whether I want to work here any longer."

As a matter of fact, this story did leak out, but not through our office. Bob Small, a reporter for the *New York Sun*, wrote it prior to any announcement, and Norton was furious.

"Your paper will fire you for that," he told Small. "They won't stand for such inaccuracies."

"I'll bet you a dinner for all the correspondents that I am

correct and that I'm not fired," Small replied. Norton, to keep up his bluff, had to take the bet, and later paid off at a dinner that Mr. Taft attended.

By this time Norton apparently had decided to fire me. He brought in W. Stoddard, an editor of the *Youth's Companion,* to study my job, but after two months Stoddard gave up in disgust and left, telling Norton that I didn't need any "editorial" help.

A little later I was in the office early one morning and just happened to glance through a stack of letters on Norton's desk. They showed that he had arranged for an increase in his own salary and in certain others, but had decided not to give me a promotion and a raise that I had been promised sometime before. I made up my mind then to have it out with him. When he came to work, I went into his office and demanded an explanation. He refused to talk about it and tried to send me back to my desk. I didn't go. A couple of Senators came by to see the President and I stood there until they had gone in and then I resumed my prodding of Norton. Other visitors came, but I just waited until they left and kept insisting on an answer. Norton became very angry, but not angry enough to carry out his threats to fire me.

There was a reason for this. The Cleveland Economy Committee, which was appointed by Mr. Taft, had been making a thorough investigation of the executive branch of the Government. The committee had given my particular job a high rating, but there was still some question about their over-all recommendations. One of the committee members, M. O. Chance, came to my defense when he learned of my difficulties with Norton, and after he had talked with the secretary, my position became less uncertain, although I did not get my promotion until sometime later.

Soon after this it was announced that Norton was resigning from the government post to become a vice-president of a big New York bank. He left without a formal farewell to the staff, but some of us knew when he was going and we managed to gather near the door. As he went out, we hummed the Doxology.

I explain the Norton episode in some detail not so much because of my personal feelings—although they were bitter at the time—but because it was a turning point in the evolution of the White House staff. The small, intimate group that had previously gathered devotedly around the President and had considered itself on familiar terms with him was never completely restored. This was not entirely a result of Norton's operations, although they delineated the change. The fact was that the office of the Presidency was becoming too big and too busy to permit continuance of the old set-up. Somewhere in Taft's administration the one-big-family atmosphere faded out, and when Woodrow Wilson became President, the times had changed and we were in a busy office that had little chance for byplay, gossip, or an occasional game of craps in the basement.

Charles Hilles, who succeeded Norton, was a remarkable man, and no secretary could have been more thoughtful of the staff. We liked him and worked hard for him, but we had been through a bad year and we couldn't swing back into the old pace. After Norton, I never called the secretaries by their first names in the office—although some of them I knew well and addressed familiarly outside the White House.

One day the Secret Service came around and showed me a couple of letters that had been passed on to them by Mrs. Taft's secretary. They were addressed to the President's daughter, Helen, and were signed by a man we will call Jones and who lived in Kentucky. He had never seen Helen Taft, but he had been reading stories about her in the newspapers and had come to the cockeyed conclusion that they were engaged to be married. The letters were written in respectful if endearing terms. The only thing wrong with them was that Jones assumed that Helen was in love with him and making wedding preparations. He added that he wanted to come to Washington to see her soon.

I took a good look at the handwriting and said I would watch for any future letters and hold them out of the family's personal mail. Another one arrived a few days later, saying Jones would be in Washington to see his "fiancée." I sent it over to the Secret Service, and not long afterward they picked up a sandy-haired, freckled little man at the White House door and brought him over to the office. It was Jones, all right. He was the most inoffensive fellow you could imagine. He was thin and not very tall, and there was a rather confused look on his face, but nothing else to suggest that he was unbalanced. He merely wanted to discuss wedding plans with his "fiancée." I pointed out to him that he had never seen Miss Taft, and that his attempts to see her were embarrassing, but he insisted that she knew all about their engagement.

"Just let me see her," he kept saying earnestly. "She knows how we love each other. She will tell you."

We got in touch with his relatives in Kentucky and found out that he was a man of some wealth. His relatives apparently didn't want to offend him, but they promised to see that he ceased writing to the White House. Either he was too smart for them or they were timid, because he made another trip to Washington, and again was sent home. His letters kept coming, and I noticed that one of them said he was sending Helen a pledge of their "engagement."

Some days later a small package arrived from a town in Ohio. It had been damaged in transit and the post office insisted that I open it and sign a receipt. It contained a diamond ring worth perhaps a couple of hundred dollars, but there was nothing to identify the sender. It was addressed to Helen and I sent it along to her. Then I got to thinking about Jones's promise of a pledge and I had it returned to me. The handwriting was that of Jones; he had tried to fool us by going over into Ohio to mail the package from an unfamiliar address. This time the Secret Service put on the pressure, and the family ended Jones's inclination to throw his money around by taking legal action to have him put away.

Meanwhile my mother had come East, and we lived in the little town of Falls Church, Virginia, about an hour's trolley ride from the White House. Washington was a slow and sleepy place in those days. Rubber-tired carriages rolled sedately along streets where the only noise was the clop of horses' hoofs, the infrequent rumble of a streetcar, or the clatter of a beer truck.

There were no movies, but there were plenty of bars with their free-lunch counters well stocked. For a quart of beer costing 5 cents you could get an excellent meal of boiled eggs, ham, cheese, and other delicacies. There was a custom in the better Washington hotels at that time that on Christmas the first drink was on the house. The usual drink was Tom and Jerry. The young blades of the town, always dressed in correct formal morning clothes, made the rounds of the hotels on Christmas morning, accumulating a sizable binge for free. This was considered a smart thing to do in those days, just as on Easter it was the smart thing to parade—and watch the parade—on Connecticut Avenue.

I may have preferred the Christmas custom at the time, but now I recall the Easter parade more clearly, perhaps for obvious reasons. I didn't take any great part in social affairs in those days, but there was a girl who lived in Falls Church whom I took to. I squired her around a bit, and she was much better than I at identifying the prominent Easter paraders. There were so many plumes waving around and so many handsome carriages on those occasions that I had only a vague notion of who was who. In fact, the profusion of plumes on ladies' hats in those days was quite a problem at the White House receptions, because they all removed their hats when they arrived and about a thousand hatboxes were needed as a regular thing.

Well, the girl was interested in such goings-on, so I took an interest in them too, and for a while I was spending less time at the bowling alley and more time on the road between my house and hers in Falls Church. This old Revolutionary town had an East End and a West End, which were about a mile and a half apart, and of course she lived at one end and I lived at the other, so that it sometimes seemed to me I was spending all my time walking that mile and a half in the evenings. This was almost too much exercise for me, and I didn't waste a lot of time before I began getting on the subject of wedding bells.

It was along about this time that I had an amusing experience, although at the time I didn't think it was funny. I don't suppose I did anything in particular to keep my fiancée from being impressed by the fact that I worked at the White House. One evening after we had become engaged, she came by the office when I was working late and expressed a desire to see the desk at which President Taft did his work. I told her that I could arrange it with no trouble at all. Then I checked around and found that everyone else had left the executive offices and I boldly led her into the President's working room.

She seemed sufficiently impressed by my influence, so I showed her around, pointing out pictures and ornaments of interest. In one corner there was a huge vase of roses, and I decided to give her one of them as a memento. When I tried to pull one out, the whole vase tumbled to the floor, spilling water on a pile of army commissions that the President had already signed—and how he hated the tiresome task of signing them!

I got the vase and the flowers back where they belonged and wiped up the floor, but when I took a good look at the stack of commissions I knew they were ruined. I thought maybe I was ruined too, because in view of the trouble I had been having with Norton it seemed likely that he would be happy to fire me if he discovered my misadventure at night in the President's office. I was plenty worried.

I removed the commissions and hid them in my desk. Then the next morning I called up the department and told them to send over duplicates. When they arrived, I merely sneaked them in with others that had come in for the President's signature, and nobody ever knew the difference. Poor Mr. Taft! He had to sign a big stack of commissions twice, but he still had me.

During the Taft administration we began to improve further the method of handling the presidential mail, especially to reduce the number of original letters that the President had to read and to save his having to read many newspapers. The method I worked out was to lay the mail out in piles, according to subject and importance, as it was being opened. Then when the opening and the reading were completed, I typed a brief of the important letters and made a list of the subjects and of the names of the writers. This list I sent to the President, and then I turned the actual letters over to his secretaries for acknowledgment or reply.

This meant that the President saw a list of perhaps sixty letters written to him, with the name and the home town of each writer and a brief description of the contents of the letter. He could quickly run through the list and familiarize himself with the correspondence in a general way, and then he could read in full any letters of particular interest to him.

I still have some of these summaries and I note the following in the list of September 28, 1910, as examples:

E. L. sends the President copies and originals of some old letters written to and by members of Lincoln's Cabinet. She also asks for the clerkship.

Solon Philbrick recommends A. K. Vickers to Supreme Court.

W. MacD. wants a job. Has been in real estate.

I. J. G. writes a would-be humorous letter of advice.

J. H. B. of Cincinnati hopes that his sister-in-law, in the Census Bureau, will be promoted.

S. K. H. of Middletown wishes the President had listened to his political advice given some time ago. Thinks the President is in a bad way.

P. S. Bullen, American representative of the *London Daily Telegraph*, wants the President to send a message by a proposed airship voyage to King George. The airship leaves Atlantic City shortly for England. Although Walter Wellman is to be on board, the writer thinks that the trip will be a success.

Mrs. O. of Bridgeport, Conn., wants to know if the President was in the White House between Sept. 1st and 15th. The husband of her niece claims that he was introduced to the President in the Blue Room sometime during that period. She thinks that the man is a liar and that he has squandered his mother-in-law's money as well.

An old ex-slave, now blind and poor, sends in his bill of sale because his old master once said: "These might some day be of use to you. He wants help; doesn't specify what.

In addition to this daily summary I compiled the so-called "yellow journal," which was made up of long sheets of paper on which were pasted news articles and editorials that might be of interest to the President, thus relieving him of the necessity of plowing through the various newspapers. I also kept a ledger in which I recorded the letters that were forwarded to the various governmental departments for answer and in this administration I took over the handling of all packages and periodicals. My job, which had started out on a small scale, was becoming so big that it kept me working many times until far into the night.

Another thing that added to my work in those days was the picture-post-card craze. This actually began back in the McKinley administration when Americans traveling in Europe began sending back post cards to friends in the United States. The President, of course, received a great many of the most elaborate cards, and some of them were really works of art. Lots of them, however, were crude affairs something like a cartoon. The craze rapidly spread and we received them from all over this country as well as from abroad.

Persons who sent post cards in those days, however, seemed to have no more to say than persons who send post cards today, so that the messages scribbled on them were of secondary importance, to say the least. As a result no one at the White House was much interested in the fact that Cousin Sue "wishes you were here," and we tossed them aside for the most part. I used to have a large box in which I dropped such cards, and eventually it occurred to me that they might be a valuable collection after a number of years. I kept on saving them until one day I examined the box, which was in the basement, and discovered that mice had eaten away what might have been a rich cache.

After Franklin Roosevelt came to the White House, incidentally, all picture post cards and greeting cards except those from personal friends were stored away and later sent to children's hospitals, where the children cut out the pictures to paste into scrapbooks as a part of the therapeutic treatment.

Mrs. Taft was one of the women for whom the White House proved disappointing. She was able and ambitious, with a keen knowledge of political methods. Her husband's inclination was toward the law courts, but Mrs. Taft had her eyes on the White House. She arrived, therefore, as a "power behind the throne," and she seemed to take that responsibility very earnestly. The Tafts loved to entertain, but within a year or so Mrs. Taft was stricken by an illness that affected her speech, and she was forced to curtail her activities.

One of the most talked-about affairs given by the Tafts was in celebration of their silver-wedding anniversary. Preparations for the party, which was to be held on the White House lawn, were discussed in great detail in the newspapers, and there was some feeling that the occasion was being overdone. Gifts came in from all over the world, many famous personages sending tokens of their esteem.

I have a list of the silver gifts from this country alone that covers twenty-one typewritten pages, and records more than three hundred doners, who sent items ranging from umbrella handles to elaborate tea sets. When everything was counted up, the gifts included 131 silver dishes and bowls, and almost as many vases and pickle forks. It seemed unlikely the Tafts would be able to make use of all of them, but they made a wonderful display of gleaming silver.

The lawn party was lavish, with a banquet that included

$500 worth of the President's favorite filet mignon. Five hundred dollars bought a lot of steak in those days. The Marine Band furnished music, and everybody had a wonderful time, especially the President.

The Tafts were probably the most brilliant and lavish entertainers, but of course every administration has had its gay parties at the White House. There were, normally, four regular receptions—the diplomatic, judicial, Army and Navy, and Congressional—each winter season. Before World War I these were brilliant affairs, especially the diplomatic reception, where there was a lavish display of gold braid, ribbons, decorations, and jewels.

In the old days, a large amount of food and liquor was served at receptions, all of it paid for out of the President's private purse. This became quite a drain on finances because of a large number of gate-crashers. In Mr. Taft's day, Congressmen especially took advantage of the occasion to bring along their political friends and guests to see the show. The ushers had orders not to admit persons without individual invitations, but of course they were not going to turn away a Congressman's half-dozen extras. There might be 2000 or 3000 persons at these receptions, a considerable part of them uninvited, but all of them eating heartily.

Lavish entertaining of this sort was suspended during World War I and as Washington's official family grew, was never resumed on the same scale. The Franklin Roosevelts did some large-scale entertaining for a while, but without the huge amounts of food and drink.

Invitations to White House affairs were usually prepared

by several expert penmen, who during the social seasons worked at nothing but filling in names of guests on engraved invitations to teas, garden parties, dinners, and receptions. This was done so skillfully that the guest's name appeared to be part of the engraving and it was difficult to tell that it had been written in by hand. For many years reception invitations were delivered by messenger, but as the list of eligibles grew it became necessary to resort to the mails, and this intimate touch became a thing of the past.

At one time, these arrangements were under direction of Colonel Crook, the disbursing officer, who was extremely meticulous and watched everything that went out from the White House with an eagle eye. One young social secretary, who was also an expert penman, made up a special invitation that he altered slightly to make it read that a reception would be "hell" at the "White Horse." This was placed with the regular invitations so that Crook would believe the engravers had made the error in all the cards. The result was a near case of apoplexy until the Colonel was finally convinced it was a joke.

Near the end of his term, Mr. Taft was thoroughly disgusted with the manner in which the President had to put up with a horde of office-seekers. He also was dismayed as a result of his split with Theodore Roosevelt, which he seemed never to understand and which he always sought to heal. During the 1912 campaign he became more and more discouraged, until the morning after election disclosed that he was third in a three-cornered race, winning the electoral votes of only Vermont and Utah. Then, of all times, he perked up.

He was both more tranquil and more jovial than at any other time he was in the White House. The strain semed to be lifted from him.

One day he sat down and wrote a pleasant letter to the man who would take his place—a letter that seems almost impossible in these days when a President is in contant danger of going broke on what was a $75,000-a-year salary.

"You will find," he wrote to Woodrow Wilson, "that Congress is very generous to the President. You have all your transportation paid for, and all servants in the White House except such valet and maid as you and Mrs. Wilson choose to employ. Your flowers for entertainments and otherwise are furnished from the conservatory and if they are not sufficient there is an appropriation from which they add to the supply. Music for all your entertainments is always at hand by the Marine Band. Provision is made by which, when you leave in the summer, you may, at government expense, take such of the household as you need to your summer home and the expense of their travel and living is met under the appropriation.

"Your laundry is looked after in the White House, both when you are here and when you are away. All together, you can calculate that your expenses are only those of furnishing food to a large boarding house of servants and to your family, and your own personal expenses of clothing, etc. This, of course, makes the salary of $75,000, with $25,000 for traveling expenses, very much more than is generally supposed.

"I have been able to save from my four years $100,000.

I give you these personal details as I would have liked the same kind of information when I came in."

Even up to the day he left, however, Mr. Taft failed to show any particular interest in the White House staff—not even the casual but warm friendliness that he showed me a few years later when I met him by chance in the park. On the final day, we were all told that we were to assemble at 11 A.M. to say good-by to the President. We did. It was typical that he had other things to do and kept us waiting until 5 P.M. When we finally filed into his office he stood up and let his eyes range over us with deliberation, almost as if he didn't know us—as perhaps he didn't. His cheeks puffed out, and he exclaimed:

"*Well!* I didn't know there were so many of you. . . . Good day!"

He carefully put on his hat and walked out of the executive offices for keeps.

Woodrow Wilson brought an entirely changed atmosphere into the White House. Whereas Mr. Taft had frequently fallen asleep in the middle of the day's business—at his desk, at a public affair, or while signing commissions—the new President was intense, alert, and always on the job.

## CHAPTER SIX

WOODROW WILSON HADN'T BEEN IN THE WHITE HOUSE A week before a plot was being hatched against him in the executive offices. It was a friendly plot, however, and the idea was to keep him from wasting his time on routine work that somebody else could handle.

I don't want to give the impression that Mr. Wilson was a slave to his desk, because he wasn't—at least not in those days. Although energetic and businesslike, he believed a man needed a certain amount of intellectual recreation, and he didn't let the job of being President crowd other things out of his life. But at first he found it difficult to adjust himself to the complicated and confusing machinery of the White House offices. He brought into his private office an old-fashioned Hammond typewriter, which had an unorthodox keyboard and made a peculiarly disagreeable tapping noise when he used it. He would walk past a secretary's desk, notice an unanswered letter or a document, and carry it back to his office. We were likely to find him later sitting at his typewriter pecking away at an answer or a memorandum that should have been handled by the secretary without any reference to the President.

He knew shorthand, and frequently made his own notes during conversations and transcribed them later, although he needed only to press a button to have such work done by an expert stenographer. After a while we began hiding papers of secondary importance from him and avoiding reference in his presence to a great many matters that could be handled by the staff. I think he soon caught onto our conspiracy, but he took it smilingly and without comment. Mr. Wilson took a number of things without comment during the years he was in the White House, but not all of them with a smile. Sometimes he was a very stubborn man. He was also the first Democratic President since I had begun handling the White House mail, and I was not sure at first that I could hang onto my job. But I did.

As we got to know the President better we were more and more impressed by his coldly logical mind and by his determination. Mr. Wilson, like Theodore Roosevelt, had to run the whole show himself. He could not work with men who disagreed with him on important matters and he got rid of them—even Colonel House eventually—whether they were clerks or Cabinet members.

Perhaps the most interesting instance was that of William Jennings Bryan, who disagreed with Mr. Wilson's policy regarding war with Germany. Bryan was an almost unbelievable character as Secretary of State, a man who was, I thought, far beyond his depth in that job even with the President himself handling all important matters.

I remember the first time I saw Bryan was at a political rally in Ohio when he was running for the Presidency. I listened to his speech as if every word and every gesture were a revelation. It is not my nature to be awed by a famous name, but I felt that Bryan was the first politician I had ever heard speak the truth and nothing but the truth. I went away convinced that he should be President. It was the next day before I began to react. I read the speech in the newspaper, and I disagreed with almost all of it when I saw it in print. I finally decided that I had fallen under the spell of the most remarkable orator of the century, which I still believe to be correct. If Bryan could have made a radio speech on election eve and every voter had been forced to listen, I think he would have won in a walk. Fortunately, there were no radios in those days, and history got one more lucky break.

It was after Bryan became Secretary of State that I observed how shallow he really was as a statesman. He would stride into our offices, a smile on his wide lips, and go in to see the President—usually to discuss petty political affairs instead of the state of foreign affairs, which were rapidly heading for a grave crisis. He scribbled memoranda to the President on scraps of paper, which he sealed in envelopes and sent to our office. I remember a typical one, written in pencil on the back of an old envelope, that said so-and-so "deserves appointment in the Postal Service because he will be able to influence a large number of voters in his community." This was at a time when war was raging in Europe and we were almost in it. Bryan was out when we did get in.

The fact that Mr. Wilson insisted on running a one-man

show did not mean that he was intolerant of the opinion of others. His methods were well illustrated by one interview he had with a group of Congressmen soon after he became President. I was in his office when the delegation arrived, smiling and enthusiastic about some legislation for which they were seeking Mr. Wilson's support. The President apparently knew nothing about the legislation and very little about the subject, but he listened attentively until they had finished and then he walked around to stand before them.

He began asking questions that were direct and squarely on the target. He pulled no punches and paid no heed to political angles. The Congressmen answered, sometimes hesitantly and sometimes squirmingly. Mr. Wilson reminded me of nothing so much as a skilled, nerveless surgeon using a knife with scientific precision. Quickly and logically, he demolished their carefully prepared argument, and although they were crestfallen when they departed, they were in no position to disagree with him.

In contrast to the President was his jovial, political-minded secretary, Joseph Tumulty. It was Tumulty who kept the place alive and moving, and sometimes in turmoil, especially when he was scouring the various branches of government to find jobs for his friends. With a fellow like Tumulty, that meant a lot of jobs.

He loved a practical joke, and frequently the staff suffered the consequences. One clerk, who became irritated by a women's-suffrage parade in front of the White House, was arrested because he seized a placard and tore it up. Tumulty, willing to see others go to any length for a joke, refused to answer his telephone calls from the police station and let him languish in jail all day before he finally identified him and secured his release. There was a lot of laughter around the office that day about Charley sitting down there in a cell.

Tumulty loved to tell stories in dialect, and to call a friend on the telephone and imitate someone's voice. Once he hid a bottle of whisky in the handbag of one of the clerks who was about to leave for the day, and then accused him of trying to steal White House property. They got into a long and loud argument in the middle of the offices as Tumulty demanded that the clerk open the bag and the clerk refused. Everybody finally caught on that it was just a gag, and it was a lot of fun—until Tumulty discovered the clerk had walked off with his own bottle of whisky!

I always had a warm spot in my heart for Tumulty because of his attitude toward an incident that involved me directly. One day Senator Ollie James of Kentucky came by the office and gave us what he said was a red-hot tip on the next day's races. He also advised us that if we went to a certain tavern on the road to Baltimore we could get better odds than elsewhere. The next day was Saturday, and Clarence Hess and I went down to the tavern on the interurban, and not only did we get good odds, but the horse James had touted won. We then bet on the next race, but about that time the telegraph wire bringing in the results failed and we were told to come in the next day to collect, in case we had picked a winner. The next morning I saw in the newspaper that my horse had won, so I went down to collect and to try to pick another one.

While I was there the place was raided by the police, who had a long string of streetcars lined up outside and took everybody to the Annapolis jail, where we were held as witnesses. "Everybody" included a number of Congressmen and some more or less important government officials. The telephone rang like mad all night as nervous politicians summoned help and bondsmen. When we got out on bail the next day, I noticed with anxiety that my name, but not any reference to the White House, was in the newspapers in connection with the raid. I rather expected Tumulty to be concerned about it when I went back to work, but he didn't say a word. He just grinned at me, and I knew that he was aware of what had happened but wasn't going to do anything about it.

Soon after Mr. Wilson became President I began to notice his correspondence with Mrs. Mary Hulbert Peck, which eventually became a choice item with the rumormongers of the day. The President had become acquainted with her sometime before, and had visited her home in Bermuda. He wrote to her occasionally—perhaps once every two months—after he came to the White House. The first letter from Mrs. Peck was opened in my office, and I read it and sent it on to the President. It was obvious that they were personal friends, and as other letters arrived I merely glanced through them at first to be sure there was nothing for the office to handle. Later I sent them to the President unopened, although he never suggested that I do so.

Soon rumors began to spread about a romance between Mr. Wilson and Mrs. Peck, and eventually some of the newspapers began to take note of the rumors, hinting that the President had gone to Bermuda especially to see her. Mrs. Wilson was ill at the time, and the gossip became so widespread that her pastor, the Reverend Dr. Beach of Princeton, N.J., finally wrote to the President. Addressing him as "Dear Woodrow," Dr. Beach called attention to the rumors and asked the President's permission to refute publicly such scandalous talk.

The President's well-known stubborn streak, however, stopped any such public statement. He replied pleasantly but firmly that the rumors were ridiculous and that it was beneath his dignity to pay any attention to them. He didn't, either, and neither the letter from Dr. Beach nor the President's reply was ever made public, so far as I know.

There was no doubt in my own mind that the friendship between Mrs. Peck and the President was on a purely intellectual level. There was unquestionably a congenial and happy meeting of minds in their correspondence, but not only could Mrs. Peck's letters have been read by Mrs. Wilson, they probably were. The gossip finally died out for lack of fuel, but it was typical of the President that he ignored it all along and kept on corresponding with Mrs. Peck.

During the Wilson administration when the President's daughter Jessie was to be married, there were, of course, many articles about and pictures of the bride in the newspapers. There were also many wedding gifts coming into the White House, but the most unusual one was an expensive monogrammed silver service. It was addressed to the bride, but there was no indication of the sender's identity. It was, however, accompanied by a gold card on which was engraved the statement: "To the most lovable girl in the world."

The gift was a great mystery to the President's household. Then one day I got a letter from a woman who had a complaint. She said that her husband had fallen in love with Miss Wilson's photograph and had taken all of their savings, which amounted to about $600, in order to send a wedding present. The wife had nothing against Miss Wilson, and in fact wished her great happiness, but she did need the money and wanted us to do something about it. The husband apparently didn't want anything except to send a gift to the bride. We connected the letter up with the mystery gift, and the silver service was returned to the shop from which it came, but I don't know whether the wife ever got her money back.

The Wilson household ran smoothly and pleasantly in the beginning, with the first Mrs. Wilson devoting herself to making everything as easy as possible for her husband. The President completely dominated their home life, in a sedate and kindly manner. He did not let the burden of high office monopolize his attention, but spent a good part of his time with his family, often reading aloud to them in the evenings.

There were those who believed that Mrs. Wilson's opposition to the marriage of their daughter Eleanor to William G. McAdoo contributed to the illness that preceded her death after a year and a half in the White House. McAdoo was then Secretary of the Treasury and was much older than Eleanor, although he retained a youthful zest and enthusiasm. After Mrs. Wilson's death the President seemed to lose some of his sprightliness until he met and fell in love with Mrs. Edith Galt. Against the wishes of his advisers, he announced their engagement on October 6, 1915.

The announcement, which the President refused to delay until after the 1916 election campaign, brought lots of mail to the White House, but Mr. Wilson was not interested. He was too much in love. There were many letters expressing indignation or disappointment that he was engaged to be married again only a little more than a year after the death of his first wife. But there also were lots of letters of congratulations and good wishes.

The debate over women's suffrage was raging then, and the second Mrs. Wilson was responsible for bringing a woman clerk into the White House office for the first time since I had been there. She persuaded the President to appoint Mrs. Maude Rogers, who had previously been employed in the Galt jewelry store in Washington. I believe all of the office force resented the appointment and looked forward to trouble. That attitude soon changed. Mrs. Rogers was one of the best and most likable employees in the office, and she stayed on long after the Wilson administration.

Mr. Wilson never took much interest in the general run of the mail coming into the White House. The trend of opinion as reflected in letters or the arrival of gifts was of no particular importance to him. His attitude was that he did not want anyone to give him "even so much as a cold potato." The rest of his family took much the same attitude, and after his second marriage this led to a peculiar little mystery. Since nobody seemed to care, it had become customary for some of the ushers and servants in the White House to divide up gifts of food and fruit that came to the President. So far as I know, there was no objection to the practice, and of course all such gifts had always been acknowledged by the office before they were sent to the White House living quarters.

On one occasion, however, Mrs. Wilson sent over to me a note from one of her friends in Virginia which referred to the fact that he had sent her some grouse, ham, and sausage, of which she was particularly fond. She asked why she had never received the food. I showed her that the food had arrived, according to my records, and had been delivered to the living quarters. We traced it that far and then it seemed to vanish into thin air. I could guess what had happened, but the food never was found and nobody ever admitted having received it in the kitchen, presumably because it had long since been eaten. Mrs. Wilson was more than a bit miffed.

The years of World War I, of course, brought many changes around the White House. The war forced expansion of the staff and we began to lose the informality of the previous administrations because the business of the Chief Executive was getting bigger all the time. The mail deliveries were getting bigger, too.

In 1914, very few persons in the United States had any idea that our country might be embroiled in the European conflict, and the mail reflected the strong opinion that what was happening abroad was none of our business. There were, of course, many hundreds of letters urging some kind of aid to one side or the other, but very few favoring participation in the war. Mr. Wilson made much of the slogan "He kept us out of war" in his campaign for re-election in 1916.

But the change that was taking place began to be seen in

the mail after 1916, and especially after the sinking of the *Lusitania.* In sharp contrast to the situation existing during World War II, there was a broad division of opinion in this country early in the war of 1914–18. It was reflected right in the White House offices, where staff members of German descent were naturally partial to the Fatherland of their ancestors and did not hesitate to speak their mind early in the conflict. The Allied Powers, however, made great propaganda use of the sinking of the *Lusitania,* and almost immediately the situation began to change. There continued to be a steady stream of antiwar mail, but this was greatly outnumbered by letters condemning the Germans and, finally, by a stream of mail favoring military action if necessary. Almost overnight the pro-Germans on the White House staff—who were good Americans first of all—were silent.

This propaganda mail greatly increased the burden of my office, and I was forced to turn over the editing of the "yellow journal" to another clerk and to get assistance to carry on my regular duties in periods of pressure. When the President finally asked for a declaration of war, the mail load reached a peak for those times, and it never did drop back to the leisurely pace of earlier days.

There was one incident about this time that I shall never forget. A brilliant young Harvard graduate who was a conscientious objector spent weeks trying to get the attention of the President in an effort to get into the diplomatic service, and thus escape being drafted by the Army. The young man had made various efforts to get a post through the State Department, and was eligible for a job, but due to a series of complicated events he had finally been turned down, and his only hope lay in an appeal that would bring a direct recommendation from the President.

He had completely failed to reach Mr. Wilson, and someone to whom he appealed finally suggested that he come to see me, because I might be able to get a letter to the President for him. I would not have done such a thing under any circumstances, but he could not realize that, and one Sunday night in the midst of a blizzard, he set out for my home in near-by Virginia.

The storm was so severe that transportation was disrupted. The boy walked several miles through slushy snow. He got lost. He was almost frozen when he appeared, covered with sleet, at my door. There were tears in his eyes as he explained the purpose of his visit and then pleaded with me to help him. I was amazed when he said that all he wanted me to do was tell him the "secret mark" to put on an envelope in order to be sure that it reached the President personally. Who had told him such a ridiculous story about a "secret mark" I never discovered, but if it had not been such a tragic event I would have found the idea highly amusing. I liked him very much and considered him a brilliant young man, but all I could do was to explain that no such thing as a secret marking on the presidential mail existed. He eventually gave up and went home. He spent the war days in jail, and I always regretted the waste of such exceptional talents as he possessed.

The war years took a heavy toll of Mr. Wilson's strength, but when the Armistice came we all felt, mistakenly, that we had come to the end of our troubles.

The so-called false armistice came along several days before the agreement for cessation of hostilities was actually signed. When the newspapers carried the story, we knew at the White House that the negotiations were in progress, and that there had not yet been any actual signing. We tried to make that clear to the reporters, but it was too late to restrain the public generally. There was a great spontaneous outburst. People paraded through the streets. The bars served free drinks. Girls whirling along the street kissed bystanders indiscriminately. Clarence Hess and I said, "What the hell! We know it's not true, but there's no point in missing the fun," so we went out and joined in. Hess kissed the girls. I had a couple or three drinks for free. It was more exciting than when the real signing came along a few days later.

While Mr. Wilson was in Europe for the peace conference, there was a great deal of suspense at the White House—and a great deal of mail, too. The mail demonstrated that most people did not understand the League of Nations, but they were very strongly in favor of the President's objectives.

The President was enthusiastic and excited when he returned home. He was pleased, too, and felt that he had achieved his objectives. Even before he had taken off his hat he came into the offices and shook hands with each of us, which was probably the most warmth he had shown us since he became President. His bearing gave us all a lift. We felt that here was a man who had willingly thrown dice with destiny, had won a victory, and had listened to the acclaim of Europe, without losing his head. He had come back and shaken our hands even before he took off his hat, in order to prove, I think, that a man need not forget where his feet were planted even though he had stood in the high places. He seemed to need to prove it not so much to us as to himself.

We felt very close to Mr. Wilson in those days, and he never lost his faith in the ultimate wisdom of the people, although there was little time left for his hopes of success. Senator Lodge began to peck at the peace structure that the President had foolishly believed he could create almost singlehanded. As the weaknesses began to appear, that inimitable obstructionist, Senator Borah, started a nationwide speaking tour against the League, in collaboration with Senator Johnson of California. No man could attack more efficiently or viciously than Borah, and soon the President's satisfaction was replaced by despair, and he decided to carry the fight to the people on a speaking tour. This tour was cut short by his illness.

When they brought him back to the White House after he was stricken while campaigning for the League of Nations, it was known only that the President was suffering from a collapse that somewhat restricted his schedule. It was several days later that we began to hear rumors that he was completely paralyzed. The official bulletins and newspaper stories, however, merely said that he was suffering from a nervous breakdown and was very sick.

In my office it became apparent that Mr. Wilson was in a far more helpless condition than was officially admitted. Since his return to Washington we had been sending documents requiring his signature to his private quarters and they had been slow in coming back. Now they ceased to come back at all. Even emergency letters that went to the White House seemed merely to vanish. When we asked about them, there was no reply.

Tumulty, of all men at the White House, was presumably closest to the President, but he had no explanation for the delay. He inquired of Mrs. Wilson and of Admiral Cary Grayson, the President's physician, but they put him off. I was directly concerned, because documents and letters continued to come to my desk and inquiries were piling up as to when some action would be taken on important matters requiring Mr. Wilson's signature. I watched Tumulty grow more and more worried. He walked from office to office, picking up papers and putting them down again. He talked to important visitors, stalling them off with vague explanations. Finally, it became obvious that Tumulty was as much cut off from the President as any of us.

Admiral Grayson was very close to the President. He had accompanied him to Europe, and he had told me how Mr. Wilson would return to his hotel suite in the evening and pace the floor, going over in great detail all the conferences of the day and repeating the conversation of each participant. Grayson would take notes as he talked and then go immediately to dictate a full report to a secretary.

I knew Grayson well, because he was a breeder of race horses and I had often gone with him to the race tracks. The next time he appeared at the offices, I made a point of running into him in the hall. I inquired about the President and got a vague reply.

"Well," I said, "perhaps I can ask you about this. I just received a personal letter for the President and I don't believe anyone else can handle it. There are some other matters in the same category. What do you think I should do?"

Grayson thought for a minute and said, "Send the letter to me over at the House"—the White House living quarters—"and I'll talk to Mrs. Wilson and see what we can do."

I avoided telling Tumulty anything about the conversation, but I sent the letter over to Grayson. Later, I sent other letters and documents directly to him. If Tumulty discovered my action, he never said anything to me. His own efforts to see Mr. Wilson were rebuffed and he was very uncertain of his position.

At this time, a letter came to the President from Judge Learned Hand of New York. It enclosed a letter signed by Bruce Bielaski, who had been head of the Bureau of Investigation of the Department of Justice. Bielaski's letter concerned grave charges against a high official in the Wilson administration in connection with the handling of property during the war. I knew that it was a matter to be taken directly to the President, but under the circumstances I was not at all certain how that was to be done or whether it was worth while to try. Finally, after I thought everyone else had gone home, I showed the letters to Charley Swem, the President's personal stenographer, and asked his opinion. While Swem was reading them, Tumulty unexpectedly wandered into the room and paused to read over Charley's shoulder. He read only a few lines and then reached for the letters.

"Let me have those," he said.

Swem held onto them. "No," he replied, "I'm handling this."

He tried to jerk away, but Tumulty was a bigger man and he had a good grip on the letters. There was a brief, brisk struggle and Tumulty pulled the letters out of Swem's hand, turned quickly, and walked into the Cabinet Room. I went down to the telephone switchboard, which was near the end of our office, and watched the operator connect the Cabinet Room phone with the Department of Justice. Five minutes later the head of that department hurried into the offices and went directly to the Cabinet Room to join Tumulty. What disposition was made of the letters I never knew.

Mr. Wilson never returned to his office. After a few weeks in which our business came to a standstill as far as it concerned matters requiring the President's personal attention, there was a demand by members of Congress for an investigation as to whether the President was incapacitated, which would have meant that Vice-President Marshall would take over his duties temporarily. Mrs. Wilson and Admiral Grayson never admitted that he was incapacitated, but for a period of about a month almost no one else—not even Tumulty—saw Mr. Wilson, and he was unable to sign his name.

Grayson later told me of a conversation he had with the President following the first grave attack. He intimated that Mr. Wilson asked him to promise that he would never disclose to the public the gravity of his condition, presumably because he hoped he could carry through the fight for the League of Nations and felt that the facts about his illness might weaken his influence. This attitude led to many wild rumors about his mental as well as his physical condition, but Grayson and Mrs. Wilson ignored them for the most part.

It appeared to us in the office that the President was unquestionably unable to carry out the duties of his office as set forth in the Constitution, but by the time a committee from the Senate was successful in its insistence upon seeing Mr. Wilson, he was able to sit up, and had begun to scribble his signature on certain documents.

Slowly, very slowly, the machinery of the White House office began to move again. Tumulty never admitted how completely he had been severed from connection with the President, but even after Mr. Wilson was able to leave his bed for short periods, Tumulty continued to send papers to Mrs. Wilson, who discussed them with the President and returned them with notations or a signature. It seemed improbable that Mr. Wilson improved very much in the year and a half that he remained in the White House.

In that year and a half the political wheel was turning back toward a new Republican administration that would bring in Warren G. Harding, whose handsome face concealed a surprisingly incendiary temper, and Calvin Coolidge, who never missed a trick, and became my favorite President.

After Mr. Harding was inaugurated, Mr. Wilson purchased and took with him to his home on S Street the big old open car he had used when he was President. Occasionally I saw him in the years before he died riding through the streets of the capital with a shawl around his shoulders and an expression of infinite sadness on his narrow, shrunken face.

# CHAPTER SEVEN

THE ELECTION OF WARREN G. HARDING TO THE PRESIDENCY was particularly exciting to me, and if I had known what was coming my way when he moved into the White House it would have been frightening as well.

The exciting part, of course, was that the new President came from Ohio, and I was pleased because I still had political contacts in that state, which had been the political stamping ground of my Uncle John back in McKinley's day. I had managed to hold onto my job during two terms in which the Democrats ran things in Washington, but you never could tell what would happen if another Democratic President got in. So I—mistakenly—heaved a sigh of relief when Harding was elected. As a matter of fact, I was in more hot water within the next few months than at any time while the Democrats were in power.

I believe I'd better pause long enough to explain that after my marriage we moved to Washington and then for a while we made a number of moves back and forth between Washington and Virginia. Our daughter Betty was born in Falls Church, so she, like her mother, is a Virginian. Then in 1916 we bought a home in what is now Arlington, Virginia, about three-quarters of an acre with large oak and hickory trees, and things went along pretty well.

My wife was soloist in several of the Washington churches for years. During World War I she went into government service for work of six months' duration, and stayed there for thirty-one years. We enjoyed life in a quiet way, and I managed to get in a reasonable amount of hunting and fishing and an occasional Saturday-night poker game. I remember one argument we had (en famille) at a time when I had received a small legacy, as to whether we were most in need of a small cabin cruiser for fishing on the Potomac or a grand piano. We finally compromised by getting both.

Betty was as curious as the next child, and as she got a little older she would sometimes go to the office with me on Sunday when nobody else was there. She would watch me cutting open the mail and ask me why I did that and I'd tell her that it was my job, just as the doctor's job was treating the sick or the grocer's job was selling us food when we went to the store. Not long after that I came home one day and found Betty sitting in the middle of our living-room floor with the wastebasket and the letters that had been delivered a few minutes earlier by the mailman. I should say the remains of the letters, because they were in tatters as a result of Betty's busy work with a pair of shears.

Before I could open my mouth to scold her, she looked up brightly and said: "Look, Daddy! I'm playing I'm Daddy at the office working hard." And with that she cut another letter into small pieces and dropped it into the wastebasket.

Well, as I was saying, we were doing all right when Mr. Harding was elected. There was a huge accumulation of mail for him by the time he was inaugurated, and that meant many extra hours of work for me, but I was feeling pretty good about it. Some of my relatives and a lot of my friends had come on from Ohio for the big doings, and there were busy times around the White House.

Soon after the inauguration, Harding's secretary George Christian came into my office with a worried look on his face.

"Now don't get excited, Ira," he said, "but the President wants to see you right away. Don't be upset."

I wasn't the least bit upset. Mr. Harding was from Ohio and my family had worked hard for his election. My mother had been in Washington recently and had called on the President. I had told her not to mention that I was working at the White House because I wanted to meet Mr. Harding in my own way, but I assumed that she had said something to him anyway.

I walked jauntily into the President's office and got my first look at Mr. Harding, who had just returned from a rest in Florida. He was tall and sun-tanned, and I thought I had never seen a more handsome man. My enthusiasm for the new boss suddenly soared and I smiled happily as I stuck out my hand. The President shook my hand, but he didn't smile. I never got a chance to say the things I had intended in the way of greetings and good wishes. His eyes bored into me, cold and angry. I knew suddenly that here was a man with a temper.

His left hand had been behind his back, but now he thrust it out toward me, holding a letter.

"Smith," he snapped, "did you open this?"

I immediately recognized it and nodded.

"I want you to understand one thing, Smith," he said in a cold voice. "I am President of the United States, but I also have a personal life. If you ever again open a personal letter of mine you will be looking for another job."

He turned abruptly and started back to his desk, dismissing me. It took me a few seconds to recover, but I realized that I had to talk back.

"Just a moment, Mr. President," I blurted out. "You probably don't understand the circumstances. When you came here I received a huge backlog of unopened letters for you. They had been lying around for days or weeks and nobody had done anything about them. They were finally forwarded to me from the Republican National Committee, from Marion, Ohio, from the Senate, and from Florida. A lot more have come to you here and there are around ten thousand in all. Of these, several thousand were marked 'personal.' I asked Mrs. Harding and I asked your secretaries, but they couldn't give me any guidance and I had no choice but to open them. I won't make the same mistake twice."

Mr. Harding paused and seemed to reconsider. "Well," he said in a more friendly tone, "I guess I didn't understand. Perhaps you are right."

The letter he had in his hand was from an old crony in Ohio. I had glanced at it, but it contained nothing of importance. It was merely the idea of someone else's opening his personal mail that caused the President's anger. Very few men are able to realize quickly the extent to which they sacrifice their personal freedom when they enter the White House. They soon find out, however, and the handling of their mail is one of the first ways it is brought home to them. In the case of Mr. Harding some very peculiar circumstances developed, and there were some things about the handling of his mail that he never did find out.

One morning not long after Mr. Harding became President I was going through a huge accumulation of mail when I came across a long envelope addressed to the Chief Executive in slanting, feminine handwriting. That envelope, I suppose, was one of the most explosive of the millions that I opened and read at the White House.

The postmark was New York, and the date showed it had been written before Mr. Harding was inaugurated, but there had been such a backlog of mail that I did not get through all of it for weeks. The envelope contained a long sheet of writing paper, which I glanced at hastily. Then I stopped and began reading carefully. I was not unaccustomed to opening letters from cranks, nuts, disgruntled job-hunters, or even practical jokers. But there was obviously something different about this one. It said that the writer was again appealing to Mr. Harding to keep his promise. It referred to earlier letters written to him, and it made one thing very clear: The writer was calling upon the President to acknowledge that he was the father of her infant daughter. The letter was signed by Nan Britton.

I let the letter cool on my desk while I thought it over and then I took it around to George B. Christian, the tall, dark, and handsome man who was Mr. Harding's secretary.

"I think you'd better see this one, Mr. Christian," I said. He read it through and got a bit white around the lips.

"My God!" he exclaimed. "If the President finds out we opened this he will fire both of us!"

Knowing something about Mr. Harding's temper, I felt that might well be an understatement. We both took another look at the letter. The handwriting was clear, but each line slanted upward toward the right-hand side of the page, and the language made me feel that the contents had been dictated to or copied by the writer. It was threatening, but stilted.

Christian hesitated briefly and then tore the letter into long strips, tore them again, and dropped the scraps into the wastebasket. We looked at each other in silence and went back to our desks. I was probably less disturbed than Christian. I felt then and later that there was political inspiration of some sort behind the Britton case. As everybody eventually learned, Nan Britton's story was that she became friendly with Mr. Harding while he was a member of the Senate and in the winter of 1919 she spent considerable time with him in Washington, after which she learned she was going to have a baby. Later, she told all in a book called *The President's Daughter.*

A couple of weeks after Christian tore up the Britton letter another similar envelope arrived for the President. I recognized the handwriting and didn't even open it. I tore it up and dumped it in the wastebasket. A third letter was handled in the same way.

I expected that any day we would hear from the President about the letters, but we never did. When *The President's Daughter* was published quite a while afterward it was a brief sensation, and then the fuss died out. Years later I met Christian at a small White House ceremony during the Truman administration. He had gone blind, but he immediately recognized my voice and said:

"Remember, Ira, when we tore up the President's letters?"

"I remember," I said. "You tore up the first one."

"Yes," he said, smiling, "I did. Good thing, too."

Mrs. Harding proved to be an ambitious First Lady. She had been instrumental in pushing her husband along in political affairs, having no desire to spend the rest of her life as the wife of the editor of a small Ohio newspaper. Having made the grade, she spent much time worrying about the President's political future and keeping his political fences in good repair.

By the time of the Harding administration, we didn't see a great deal of the White House family life, but Mrs. Harding was always looking in on us. Usually, she was accompanied by a group of political guests from the Corn Belt who were being given a conducted tour of the White House. Mrs. Harding would lead a frumpy-looking crowd, mostly women, into the office and start explaining things to them in the manner of a Chinatown sight-seeing-tour conductor. She never understood the workings of the office herself, so she would always bog down in the middle and say, "You tell them, Mr. Smith." Always made me wish I'd taken that afternoon off to go fishing.

Mrs. Harding's favorite around the place was a doctor who, through her efforts, became the President's physician; he also became a Brigadier General. He was a little fellow, a bit on the pompous side, and not particularly popular except with the First Lady. So on the first day he arrived in his resplendent uniform, the news photographers went to work on him. They stopped him outside the office and posed him all over the place, but particularly walking down the driveway. He strutted a bit normally, but with the uniform he strutted good. They made him do it over and over, snapping their cameras endlessly while the doctor sweated in the sun.

After about fifteen minutes, while he was panting but still game, I asked one of the boys why they were wasting so much film on him.

"Hell, we're just having fun," he replied. "Nobody's had any film in his camera since the first shot. But we like to see him strut."

Perhaps the most famous figure of the Harding days was Laddie Boy, a handsome Airedale dog that was better known in his time than even the Roosevelts' Falla. Laddie Boy was friendly, but ready to fight anything that showed up in a pugnacious mood. After Mr. Harding's death on a trip that his wife had thought would be helpful toward his renomination, the dog was given to Harry Barker of the Secret Service. Stories about Laddie Boy had helped spread the craze for Airedales at the time, and I had a fine Airedale bitch that I wanted to mate with the Harding dog. Harry refused my suggestion.

"I can't do it," he said. "Mrs. Harding made me promise

never to breed Laddie Boy, because she wanted his line to die with him. Don't ask me why."

Later, my bitch had some puppies and one of the news photographers made a cute picture of them. It was published in many newspapers with a caption that mistakenly gave the impression that they had been sired by Laddie Boy. I was deluged with letters offering big prices for the pups.

Mr. Harding's comparatively short tenure in the White House was remarkable chiefly for a lot of political hocus-pocus, and the case of the decapitated salmon. The hocus-pocus is well known, so I will mention only the salmon, which was the first big catch of the season in Maine and was sent as a gift to the President. When it arrived, one of the more publicity-minded Congressmen from Maine called up and insisted that he wanted to present it to the President, for the benefit, chiefly, of the news photographers. It was finally arranged, and he rushed down to the White House for the ceremony.

Everybody gathered around. The Congressman smoothed his hair, the photographers were summoned, and word was sent to the kitchen to produce the salmon. Then there was a delay—quite an ominous delay. Finally it developed that the cook had cut off the salmon's head because it was too big to put in the icebox before decapitation. There were wails of anguish, but there was also an inspiration. A needle and thread were found and the salmon's head was sewed on again. You'd never have guessed it when you saw the pictures.

# CHAPTER EIGHT

Calvin Coolidge was in the White House during an economic boom time when it seemed that almost everybody in the country was gambling on the market except the President and me.

Some of the White House staff bought stocks on margin. Important political and business figures, such as John Hays Hammond, were always coming into the executive offices and passing out hot tips on when to buy what and when to sell. I never took advantage of their suggestions. My job of handling the White House mail gave me access to much information that a stock-market gambler could have used to great advantage. I never used it. Others on the staff went in for real-estate gambles, and some of them urged me to participate in several deals that seemed likely to turn a quick profit. I never did.

I wouldn't attempt to guess what Mr. Coolidge thought about such goings-on, but it was always my idea that I'd rather put my money on a good horse running at Havre de Grace. My friends and colleagues frequently spoke critically of my business dealings with the race-track bookies, but in the end I think I came out about as well as the stock-market gamblers who saw their paper profits collapse in 1929 and the real-estate speculators who had their property washed down the Potomac by floods. Anyway, I had more fun.

So did Mr. Coolidge. He was never a spectacular President. Mostly he just sat tight, although I always felt that he would have been prompt and firm in any crisis. But he was best known, I suppose, for the amusing stories about him. He was built up and built himself up as a man with a steady hand and a quizzical sort of Vermont humor. It was a pretty accurate picture as far as it went, but it paid scant attention to his New England inhibitions. It always seemed to me that he suppressed his feelings to the point where he was sometimes quietly boiling inside, and when his irritation did pop out, it was in an abrupt, indirect fashion.

I came to know Mr. Coolidge unusually well. We were both careful not to make a point of our friendship, although there was one time when I very much wanted to try. That was when his son Calvin died and the President suffered a period of utmost despondency without ever permitting anyone on the outside even to attempt to help him. He went about his routine almost as usual, giving no outward sign of what I knew to be a great emotional struggle. He never mentioned the illness or the loss of his son, and never gave me or anyone else a chance to express even a word of sympathy. It made me think he might have been far better off if he could have let some emotion show through, at least for a moment.

My first contact with Mr. Coolidge was unusual. When Warren G. Harding died, Mr. Coolidge refused to move into the White House until after the funeral, which was a week or so later. He wouldn't even use the executive offices, having taken over a Willard Hotel suite that was transformed into working rooms. Mr. Coolidge had a big staff provided by the Superintendent of Buildings and Grounds, and in a few days complete chaos had been achieved both at the Willard and at the White House excutive offices.

Finally, three of us from the White House staff went down to the hotel and co-ordinated operations, and the President was not only grateful but remembered it. On the day he moved to the White House he asked all of us to come up into the Willard ballroom and had his picture taken with us.

The President followed a fairly regular daily routine, but he was in the habit of popping up at odd times in the most unexpected places, roaming from basement to attic and just looking in to see that everything was as it should be. At such times he was always asking countless questions, although in general he was impatient of anyone who wasted words or motions or failed to get his work done in orderly fashion.

I usually got to the office about 8 A.M. in order to have the mail in readiness when the staff arrived, and after the President had taken his morning walk. Along toward 8:30 I would usually see him coming back to the White House with one Secret Service man, probably Colonel Edmund W. Starling, walking beside him, and another following closely.

The President walked very straight, with his nose pointed directly forward and his hat set squarely on top of his head. But without ever turning his head he took in everything in front, to his right, and to his left—and sometimes, I think, to his rear. His eyes were constantly moving back and forth in eager and inquisitive search. On one occasion my daughter and I were some thirty feet off to one side of him as he walked stiffly down the street and I was sure that he had not seen us. But not only did he lift his hat—without turning his face toward us—but later he asked Starling many question about my daughter, where she went to school, where we lived, and so on.

When he turned into the White House grounds after his walk he would head straight for the basement driveway at a fairly fast clip. Then just as he came opposite our office door he would sometimes make a sharp right turn so unexpectedly that the momentum of the Secret Service men would carry them on to the driveway before they could stop, while the President would be entering the office alone and with a pleased expression on his face. He would walk into my office, look down his sharp nose at me, and say: "Good morning. Are there any mails for me?" Or he often asked particularly if there were "mails" from his father. I would have his personal letters ready and he would carry them off to his office. He had a thorough knowledge of the office, and would often go himself to the files for records.

On mornings when I was late to work I might find him sitting in my chair, with his feet on the desk, reading letters he had sorted out of the mail. On such occasions he would not even look at me, and instead of saying anything, I would go to another desk, sit down, and twiddle my thumbs until he decided to leave. He usually departed without speaking to me, and I felt that if I had offered any explanation of my failure to beat him to the office he would have merely sniffed and walked away.

I don't know whether the President ever sat with his feet on his own desk, but I was always glad he chose to park his shoes on mine on those occasions. I always enjoyed doing it myself, and if anybody raised an eyebrow at me I pointed out that what was good enough for Mr. Coolidge was good enough for me. I always felt that way about the Coolidge administration in general, too, because it was the most enjoyable of all from my viewpoint. Right now I feel that I never want to open another letter of any kind, but if I could work for Mr. Coolidge, I'd be happy to go back on the job tomorrow—provided both of us could get some time off for fishing.

Mr. Coolidge was a master of dry and dead-pan humor. He never smiled at his own jokes, and if you wanted his respect, you never acted more than moderately amused. He didn't face you when he was making a joke, but he always cut his eyes around to see whether you caught it. This put quite a strain on some members of the staff who either were inclined to laugh out loud, or who weren't always sure when it was a joke. I usually found his jokes of a caliber that enabled me to restrain my laughter, and we got along fine.

Once when an Ohio Congressman was making a big front-page fuss about bureaucratic wastefulness and idleness, Mr. Coolidge came into the office and saw Charley Wagner, the chief stenographer, with his feet on a desk and a newspaper opened so that his face was covered and he failed to see the

President. Mr. Coolidge walked up to him, tapped at the paper, and said severely, "That man from Ohio will get after you." Then he hurried away. Wagner never was sure whether he was being ribbed.

On another occasion the President came into the office and examined some packages that had just arrived. He was apparently about to open a big one when I reminded him that it was against Secret Service orders for the President to open any packages. He was a bit peevish about it, and since I knew what was in the package because of a letter received earlier, I told him I would open it while he watched. It turned out to be a big and costly picture frame that held a very gaudy and unattractive colored photograph of a locomotive, sent in with the compliments of the manufacturers. The President looked at it in petty disappointment, and then, cutting his eyes toward me, said:

"Well, send it over to the house. Mama can make good use of that frame."

The Coolidges had been given a big white collie after they came to the White House, and although the President didn't care much for the dog, it often went with him on his ramblings around the place. One day he investigated the White House basement's innermost recesses and came across William Pannell, a big, fast-talking Negro janitor who had quarters there. Pannell had not seen the President close up before, but he quickly leaped at the opportunity to make him feel at home in the White House, and to explain in enthusiastic terms how much he admired Mr. Coolidge.

The President listened for about thirty seconds, and made

up his mind that Pannell was building up to ask him a favor. This was a mistake, because Pannell just liked to talk, but it was a natural mistake on the part of a President who was always being asked for something. Mr. Coolidge turned abruptly away, saying "Come on, doggie," to the big collie. He walked swiftly to the door, and then turned back to the crestfallen Pannell.

"Well," he said, "take anything that isn't nailed down. . . . Come on, doggie."

He was always suspicious of politicians, but he played the game according to rules. With an eye toward the 1924 nomination he brought in Bascom Slemp, a millionaire Southern coal operator, to be his secretary. Slemp had been in Congress and was able to exert such a strong influence on his party in the Southern states that when the Republicans were in power in Washington he was called the "little President of the South."

His atention was devoted to the President's political problems, and he did a good job. Like Jim Farley, he had an excellent memory for faces and names, and a pocketful of tricks to smooth over the situation if he forgot one. Slemp arranged for the first radio broadcast ever made by a President before Congress, and Mr. Coolidge's precise New England voice went over the air waves with good results. Slemp had made sure that the greatest possible audience was listening, and after the broadcast he wrote to some of his hillbilly political friends in Tennessee and asked them to report on reaction to the speech. One of them replied: "There wasn't no reaction. Everybody liked it."

Another able aide of Mr. Coolidge was Judson Welliver, a newspaperman who did research and helped write the President's speeches. In those days the President did not have a regular press secretary or a ghost writer, and there was no provision for such an employee on the White House pay roll. Welliver was technically in the employment of another government department, but he was lent to the White House without having any official title.

He was an extraordinarily skillful writer, but he liked to take a drink whenever he was sure Mr. Coolidge would not find out that he was violating the Eighteenth Amendment. One day he waited until the President had left his office and then he dragged out a bottle of homemade wine that I had concocted and traded to him for a bottle of bourbon. Welliver preferred my wine to bourbon and was always after me to trade. He took a few drinks and was feeling no pain when Mr. Coolidge returned unexpectedly to his office and summoned his ghost writer.

Welliver went reluctantly because my wine had an aroma almost equal to its kick. He stood inside the door of the President's office.

"I wanted you to see this, Mr. Welliver," the President said in his precise Vermont voice, pointing with his finger at a newspaper. "Come over here."

Welliver moved up as far as the desk. "Yes, sir."

Mr. Coolidge looked up. "Come around here, Mr. Welliver, where you can see it."

"I can see it from here, Mr. President," Jud replied. Mr. Coolidge sniffed.

"Mr. Welliver," he said sharply, his finger still on the item under inspection, "I asked you to come around here where you can see it."

Welliver moved around the desk, trying to hold his breath. The President sniffed again, handed him the paper, and stood up.

"I'll see you at ten o'clock tomorrow, Mr. Welliver," he said sedately, and departed. He sniffed once more as he left, but he didn't say anything later to Jud.

One day the President stopped at my desk and asked me whether his son John received much mail. John was a likable and good-looking kid, and he had been getting a good deal of fan mail, especially from teen-age girls who wanted the thrill of writing to a boy in the White House. Some of these letters from girls he didn't know were clever, and occasionally John would answer one of them with a flippant note.

I told Mr. Coolidge that there were usually some letters for John every day or so. He nodded, and said that hereafter I was to send them to him instead of the boy. The next day John wandered in, acting a bit too casual. We talked about nothing much until he finally asked whether his father had given me instructions about his mail. I told him what had happened.

"Well," he said with some embarrassment, "it doesn't matter except for one thing. You see, there's one that's different. I don't mind Dad getting the others, but this one . . . You know the one I mean?"

Yes, I said, I believed I knew the one.

"You know she's an old friend, and not like the crazy ones

that just write in without knowing me. I wondered if maybe . . ."

"John," I said, "I'm sorry, but I have very definite orders from the President and you'll have to work it out with him." The boy's face showed how he felt about *that.* So I went on: "Of course you know how we do things here. I sort out your letters each morning and put them in a pile right there on the corner of my desk. Then I sort the other letters. Sometimes I even have to go out of the room for some reason or other. Then later I send the letters over to your father."

John gave me a long, pleased look and departed. The next morning I sorted out his letters, and there was one from *the* girl. I kept an eye on the door, and when I saw John coming I got up and went elsewhere. When I came back *the* letter was gone and so was John. We worked it that way for quite a while, and I don't think we ever missed a trick. I guess our little trick was all right, because later John married the girl. She was Florence Trumbull, daughter of the Governor of Connecticut.

The President was not a generous giver, but he always wanted to do the right thing. One day he walked up to my desk and suddenly handed me a box of cigars.

"Have some tobaccah," he said. Then he walked on down to the desk of Nelson Webster, the disbursing officer, and repeated the performance. Webster and I later compared notes and found that he had taken the trouble to discover what price cigars each of us smoked. Webster smoked twenty-five-centers and he got twenty-five-cent cigars. I smoked ten-centers and that's what I got. Both boxes, incidentally, came from the large number of gift cigars sent to the President that were stacked up in his study. I guess Mr. Coolidge figured that if I smoked ten-cent cigars I wouldn't appreciate anything better.

Mr. Coolidge never had a real vacation until he came to the White House, but there he learned to enjoy them. On one trip to upper New York State he tried fishing, and loved it. There were a lot of stories making fun of him for using a worm to catch trout, but actually he became quite proficient. His main complaint was that Starling, who considered himself an expert hunter and fisherman, always made him go down to Chesapeake Bay to fish, claiming that fishing was not worth while in the near-by Potomac. The President didn't like the long trip, but he took Starling's word for it. This had gone on for some time when the President came in one day and found me absent.

"Where's Rapid Transit Smith?" he asked. He never addressed me that way, but when I was not present he often referred to me as Rapid Transit because my initials are I.R.T., just like the Interborough Rapid Transit system in New York City. I think he liked that because I am a rather deliberate person.

One of the boys allowed as how I might be down on the Potomac fishing, which I was. The next day Mr. Coolidge came in early.

"Catch anything?" he asked abruptly.

I said I caught a few nice bass. He took his mail without another word and walked out. Sometime later, Starling came in with a red face and complained bitterly that I had knifed him, and said he had caught hell from the President for saying there were no fish in the Potomac.

Mr. Coolidge also tried hunting, but with unsatisfactory results. Starling took him out with a party looking for quail. They trudged along until the dogs made a point. Then everybody stepped back to let the President have the first shot. The quail were flushed and whirred away, but no shot was fired. When they looked at Mr. Coolidge he was holding the gun in the crook of his arm and watching the birds. Never did fire. Never hunted again, either.

Being a hunter myself, I enjoyed hearing about the President's attitude toward shooting, and I had a little fun with him the following Christmas as a result of an accident. I had gone hunting with Dr. Walter Bloedorn and was a little in front of him when some birds got up. We both shot, and three No. 8 chilled shot from his gun struck my cheek. He was distressed, and insisted on going back to a farmhouse, where he picked out the shot and dabbed my cheek liberally with iodine. As I had previously scratched my other cheek on some bushes, he completed the job by using the iodine on spots all over my face.

The next day was Christmas, always a rush time in the mail room, and I went down to the office to catch up on my work. While I was there the President came in, and he gave my splotched face a long, searching look. I knew he was curious, but I didn't offer any explanation. He fussed around for a while and finally gave me one of those sidewise glances.

"Been to a party?" he asked tersely.

I nodded. "Yes, a shooting party," I replied, just as tersely.

He looked at me questioningly, but I went on sorting the mail and didn't say any more. I knew he wasn't going to ask, either, but it was burning him up. He kept on fooling around and I kept on saying nothing. My little joke was spoiled when Bloedorn, still worried about me, came by to look at the scratches, and of course talked about what had happened. The President didn't comment, but after hearing the whole story he gave me an amused side glance, pleased that he had found out after all.

The President didn't often resent things that were amusing. There were stories at one time that he was angry because Will Rogers imitated his voice in a very clever skit on the radio. Lots of people thought it was really Mr. Coolidge, and wrote in complaining about what he said. Rogers, fearing that he had offended the President, sent him a letter of apology, and in return got a telegram inviting him to lunch at the White House. He wired back: "My God, Mr. President, do you really mean it?"

The President was always much interested in the gifts that came to him, and he kept a close check on them, but he was also careful about government property. Two incidents illustrate this attitude.

Two weeks before the then Prince of Wales visited the White House, his equerry came to my office and explained that the British Embassy was sending over several cases of the Prince's own Apollinaris water, which was the only water he ever drank. The equerry wanted to know how to arrange for it to be served at the table and made available in the Prince's room. I put him in touch with the steward, and in return for the favor, he sent me a case of the Apollinaris water in handsome bottles with a special label showing that it was put up by a Special Purveyor to His Royal Highness.

I was pleased, because I wanted to show off the bottles to my friends and give some of them away as souvenirs, but by mistake my case was placed with some packages for the House proper and came under the watchful eye of Mr. Coolidge. He just assumed it was for him and told the steward:

"Oh, fine. I like that size bottle. Send it right up to my study and we'll use it this afternoon for some lemonade."

Nobody wanted to dampen his enthusiasm by correcting the misunderstanding, and I had to see my prize souvenirs disappear in the direction of the President's study. But he made up for it later. One day he was talking to me about fishing and I remarked that I was going to have a new icebox made to fit into a certain place on my boat. I was planning to go down that day to get the exact measurements.

"Let me have the measurements," he said.

The next morning he asked if I had the measurements and I handed them to him on a slip of paper.

"Don't do anything until you hear from me," he said, and disappeared for half an hour. When he came back he was looking pleased. "I've got one just the right size and you can have it," he said. "All you'll have to do is saw the iron legs off."

The icebox he gave me was a handsome one that had been in his study and was being replaced by an electric refrigerator. Later, when I told him it was just right, I also asked him jokingly what he was going to do about a missing icebox when the next check-up was made on the White House inventory.

"Oh, that's all right," he said. "You can give me your old one."

Almost every White House family has some pet that becomes well known to the nation. In the case of the Coolidges, it was the handsome white collie dog already mentioned. The collie was best known, perhaps, because it was included in a portrait of Mrs. Coolidge done by Howard Chandler Christy. The President liked the painting and decided it would be nice to send photographs of it to their friends. One was sent to the man who had given the collie to the President. Mr. Coolidge got a telegram in reply: "Fine picture of dog. Send more photographs."

Mrs. Coolidge was the most charming First Lady I knew, and she was admired by all of the staff. Like the President, she took a friendly interest in us and helped make our work pleasant. The President, however, was always on guard against anything or anyone that might attract unfavorable attention toward the White House. Any breath of scandal frightened him, and he never took a chance, probably because the Harding-administration scandals were so vivid in his mind. Several White House employees who were involved in unsensational divorce actions or something of the sort were quietly but quickly shifted to other jobs. The President never waited to see whether there would be gossip; he got rid of the man if anything arose that just *might* lead to gossip.

I think that was what happened in the case of the Secret Service man who accompanied Mrs. Coolidge on her walks.

They became good friends, and Mrs. Coolidge was interested to learn that he was very much in love with a girl he later married. But somehow a small rumor started about Mrs. Coolidge and her Secret Service companion. It was the sort of thing Woodrow Wilson would have stubbornly ignored because it was so obviously false, but in this case the Secret Service man immediately vanished from the White House detail. The President of course knew that the rumor was ridiculous, but he took no chances on any fingers being pointed at the White House.

The President didn't miss any political bets either, for all of his dead-pan approach to publicity hoop-la. He had a temper that could make itself felt in high places, but he always felt a strong sympathy for the ordinary citizen and frequently went out of his way to perform some little act of thoughtfulness for a stranger.

One Sunday morning when I was at the office trying to catch up with a heavy flood of mail he came over from the White House and stood beside my desk while I opened a large pile of letters. One of them was a special delivery letter from a woman who wanted to know what church the President would attend that day and at what time he would be there. She explained that she was in Washington only for a few days and that she wanted her small son to get a glimpse of the President while he was in the capital because it would be something he would remember always and could tell his friends about. She asked whether it would be possible to telephone her at her hotel and tell her which church Mr. Coolidge would attend.

I handed him the letter and he read it carefully. Without

saying anything, he picked up a pencil and wrote: "Phone 10:30 A.M. Monday." He handed the notation to me and went abruptly away. Such notes were typical of Mr. Coolidge, and I understood that he meant for me to telephone the woman and tell her to bring her son to the White House on Monday at 10:30 A.M. for a visit with the President. This I did, and the delighted mother and son were received by Mr. Coolidge.

When Mr. Coolidge's term ended, he just sort of faded out of the White House without any formal good-bys, and Herbert Hoover took over. I, for one, was sorry to see Mr. Coolidge go, because it seemed to me that his departure marked the end of a chapter in our history. He was probably the last of our modern-era Presidents who was able to give the impression of avoiding the extreme mental and physical strains of the office. This was due both to the period in which he served and to his temperament, although it was difficult to tell just what tensions were at work behind that New England façade.

He believed, however, that a man was inefficient if he failed to get through his allotted work each day. Mr. Coolidge always got through his. He didn't like noise or hoop-la, and he didn't like sudden and drastic changes—the kind of changes that we were heading for even if we could not then see them. He was, perhaps, a little old-fashioned, and, as I hope I've made clear, I liked him, and I believe he liked me. I never laughed heartily at his jokes—just enough to let him know I got the point. He seemed to like that. He may even have realized that very few of his jokes were worth more than a mild chuckle, but I doubt it.

# CHAPTER NINE

WHEN HERBERT HOOVER BECAME PRESIDENT THE COUNTRY was in the midst of a prosperous and booming time, but it was also a time of ferment and change and underlying restlessness. Things were never going to be the same again in the U.S.A., and especially not in the White House.

It always seemed to me that in the late nineteen-twenties the country tended to go a bit wacky about science. Now don't get me wrong; I'm a great advocate of scientific progress. What I mean is that you sometimes got the impression that people believed science could make up a few formulas, push a few buttons, and solve all the problems of the world. Those were the days when everybody was reading with avid excitement books about how things were doing in outer stellar space and people were gabbing about Einstein's discoveries in the electromagnetic-gravitational field as if they understood what it was all about.

I always encouraged such people to go on learning, but they reminded me of the horse players who had worked out a perfect system for cleaning up at the track. I never felt they knew exactly what they were talking about. My own hunch was that running the world would continue to be a job calling for a lot of hard work, and that picking the winners would call for considerable knowledge of horseflesh, track conditions —and luck.

This scientific trend I mention not disparagingly, but because it properly coincided with the administration of Mr. Hoover, who was hailed as the Great Engineer. I think people may have had a feeling that the country was running a little wild economically, but that if they elected Mr. Hoover, his scientific genius would straighten things out and the people could go on doing as they pleased.

As far as the White House was concerned, Mr. Hoover brought about some changes, and was the originator of the multiple-secretary system. His engineering mind was inclined to put everything into the proper pigeonhole, including the staff, and his political, press, and executive secretaries formed a buffer line around the President day and night. Big-business methods had finally taken over at the White House. It was about time, I suppose, but it was a far cry from the days of the McKinley administration when each of us could do almost any job in the office, and when the President often answered his mail by handing a letter to some clerk and saying: "Oh, tell him thus and so. You know how to say it."

As a matter of fact, the White House staff never has been very efficient and, due to political and other considerations, it is not likely that it ever will be. Sometimes, of course, it has been highly inefficient, and there have been periods of slipshod and unbusinesslike operations that would not be tolerated in private business. There have also been furious outbreaks in which commissions and efficiency experts did their stuff zealously, but they have never made more than moderate progress in ending duplication of work and the rivalries of various divisions that interfered with our operations.

In my own job of handling the mail, I did a major part of the actual work myself for many years, getting assistance assigned to me only during periods of heavy mail deliveries, such as the inauguration of a new President or debate over some vital issue in national or international affairs. The need for help arose in the Wilson administration, but it slackened off some early in the nineteen-twenties, and the volume did not permanently become heavy until the Hoover administration, which was the beginning of the modern period of big-scale presidential mail.

After I had begun to acquire a force of clerks on my own staff, I tried to develop in each administration systems for handling the mail that would fit in with the practices of other government divisions, particularly the divisions to which we necessarily had to forward much of the White House mail. This effort frequently backfired in the complex bureaucratic system that has grown up in Washington, because others took the position that we were trying to assume too much responsibility, or that we were delegating disagreeable work to other divisions when we might be doing it ourselves. I spent a lot of time trying to keep our relations smooth so that we could get the co-operation of other divisions in handling the growing volume of mail.

Another difficulty was that until 1946 only a few clerks were appointed by Executive Order to the White House rolls. The great majority of the force was detailed for an indefinite period from various other departments of the Government. That is, most of the persons working at the White House actually were technically in the employment of other departments, such as Interior or Treasury, and were paid by appropriations Congress made for these other departments, which then detailed or lent them to the White House.

Whenever we needed additional clerks we would send a statement of requisite qualifications to one of the departments and ask for a certain number to be detailed to us. In such cases, however, the White House did not normally put on pressure for well-qualified clerks, and we were likely to get clerks that the department felt wouldn't be missed much.

I always felt this attitude was a mistake, and when additional clerks were being asked for the mail room I found excuses to designate particular persons whose ability I knew. Since the request came from the White House, they were usually made available, and I was able to keep my own staff at a high level. In fact, the greatest fault with my system was that I got some people detailed from other departments who were too good for the jobs in the mail room.

I remember way back in McKinley's time that the President's inclination to be helpful and friendly resulted in the installation of one of the most unusual ushers in White House history. He was a Swiss who spoke English in a way that very few Americans could easily understand, and he got his job only because his wife was Mrs. McKinley's personal maid and the First Lady was very fond of her. The Swiss might have been a fine usher in Berne, but his poor English made him an amusing figure in the White House, a circumstance that he never realized as he went about his duties, which included showing visitors through the famous rooms on the first floor. He always ended up by explaining a few facts about how he got his job and saying: "I feel der responsi-beel-ity of der position."

That was more than you could say for some of the persons who have drifted on and off the White House staff. I recall two boys who were assigned to me by one presidential secretary. They were his personal friends, and were bright kids. One of them turned out to be the secretary's social assistant and the other one went to law school all day and reported at the White House in the evening, just in time to study for his classes the next day. They were nice boys, but they didn't give *me* any help.

On the other hand, when commissions and experts were surveying efficiency at various times at the White House it was difficult for them to make allowances for fluctuation of work, especially in the mail room. One month there might be comparatively little to do and we would have periods of idleness. The next month we might be forced to work late every night just to keep up with the stream of mail. Thus one period usually made up for the other, and if an investigator found a clerk reading the newspaper or one of the girls doing a little knitting, it did not mean that the Government's money was being wasted. That was a situation that existed during the entire period I worked at the White House, and I imagine that it will always be more or less that way.

In general, however, we always had decent, efficient, hard-working people in the mail room, and the Government got its money's worth. Some of the clerks stepped from the White House into private industry and—with White House prestige behind them—made wonderful successes in the business world.

On the other hand, we had a few misfits. I recall one clerk with a phobia for violent exercise, which he told us took the form of swinging from tree to tree, à la Tarzan. Another was a bit overwhelmed by working at the White House, and represented himself elsewhere as an assistant secretary to the President—until he was permitted to find another job. One of the messengers who did certain errands to stores around town always sought out the proprietors and told them he was "pulling" for them to get White House orders. In that way he collected cigars, liquor, chickens, and other items that he said would be used for a party for White House clerks. He was soon permitted to depart.

One clerk fell in love with the photograph of a Congressman's daughter and wrote her passionate love letters. The Congressman got wind of what was happening and moved in rapidly, removing the clerk from the premises. There was another clerk who stuck around for a long time trying to make something out of the prestige of working at the White House. He watched carefully for Cabinet members, Senators, and other prominent visitors, and usually managed to get around to greet them while they were waiting to get into the President's office. They had no idea who he was, but he always clapped them on the back, shook their hands, and shouted, "How are you, boy!" or, "It's a great day, eh, boy!"

and of course they usually said yes, it was. The clerk worked hard at making friends in that manner for a long time, but he never did get very far and finally gave it up. It was a relief to some Senators when he departed, because they never had figured out who he was and felt embarrassed about asking.

Well, Mr. Hoover tried to make a few improvements around the place and I guess he did. So many unhappy developments came along during his term that in the end it didn't seem to matter much whether the White House staff was running efficiently; the problem was whether the country was going to keep on running at all.

The President was affable when we saw him, but that wasn't often. When he wanted something he would call us on the telephone, and his secretaries considered his time so valuable that they never let him waste it chatting with the office help. I always felt that this intense feeling of efficient and big-scale operations contributed to Mr. Hoover's political difficulties. He was a good conversationalist and enjoyed a joke when he got a chance, but it always seemed that he was too busy—or he was made to appear too busy and too efficient—ever to relax and be himself.

And of course as the country stumbled into a period of economic desperation Mr. Hoover was worried and harassed. He arranged a scientific check of the mail to watch the trend of public opinion on such matters as Prohibition, and then on the efforts that were made to combat the depression. He worried about propaganda mail without seeming fully to understand how much of it was cleverly inspired by his political foes. He was swayed by false hopes and fears, and he just couldn't seem to make up his mind. The mail for months was full of reports on bank failures and foreclosures which made it obvious that some action must be taken, yet Mr. Hoover delayed. He wanted to be *sure* before he did anything, but by that time it was usually too late to make much difference, or he was frustrated by partisan politics. He read and absorbed wonderful reports from financial advisers at home and abroad, but about all that happened was that they went into a large filing cabinet, or so it seemed to me.

His secretaries were no great help in those days. Lawrence Richey was a good man who had come up from the Secret Service, but he could never win the sympathy of the newspapermen. Walter R. Newton, the political secretary, was so ambitious in Minnesota that, according to newspaper reports, he let his own affairs interfere with the President's political welfare. Mr. Hoover, however, had implicit faith in him, and no one ever dared tell him the truth.

The President worked at a terrific pace as conditions became more critical. He was at his desk at all hours and got very little relaxation or exercise. He didn't like exercise anyway, and when he was persuaded to toss a medicine ball around in the back yard he did it in halfhearted fashion. If the ball came his way he would catch it and throw it to somebody, but he didn't make any effort to attract a toss.

It became more and more difficult for his secretaries and his doctor to get him out of the White House for a week-end rest. The Marines had built a fine camp for him on the Rapidan River, and for a time he went there with week-end guests, usually Cabinet members, whom he put to work carrying stones to build a dam. They didn't care much for such hard labor, and later Mr. Hoover went to the camp only under strong pressure.

Frequently it was announced that he would leave on Friday noon, but at 7 P.M. he would still be working at his desk. Many times he merely canceled the trip at the last minute, and we never knew for certain that he would go until his automobile had crossed the Potomac. Even then he might return the next day. This naturally made it difficult for the White House newspapermen, who never knew whether they would make a trip to the Rapidan or sit in Washington over the week end. It didn't help Mr. Hoover's press relations when they had to unpack their bags on Friday night, or when they had to make a last-minute scramble to get started.

On one occasion the correspondents had decided not to prepare for the scheduled week-end trip because the several before had been called off. Then with about half an hour to spare they were told to be ready. They had been in the habit of taking a small supply of bootleg liquor with them, because it was always a dull week end at the small hotel at Culpeper near the President's camp where they stayed. This time they were not prepared, and one of them made a hurry-up call to the bootlegger.

"Bring two gallons of alcohol and gin drops to the White House right away," he ordered.

There was a long silence on the other end of the phone, and then a startled voice said: "I can't do that. It's a penitentiary offense to take it to *your* house. God knows what it would be to take it to the White House!"

"Don't worry," the reporter said. "Just stop at the door and tell the cop . . ."

"The cop! No!"

"Look, it's all right. Tell the cop at the door that it's for me. I'll fix it."

The bootlegger agreed only after being threatened with the loss of a lucrative part of his business, and he later walked, trembling and sweating, into the executive offices with a police escort. He emptied his satchel in the pressroom and departed, quietly but unbelievingly. I'm tempted to say Mr. Hoover wouldn't have believed it either, because he knew there was a law. But I don't think that would be correct. Mr. Hoover was always well informed on Prohibition as well as other issues, and my guess is that he believed the Eighteenth Amendment to be a failure. The trouble was that his thinking always seemed—to me, anyway—to be about a year ahead of his acting.

Near the end of the Hoover administration, in the two-hundredth year after George Washington's birth, Jimmy Doolittle made an airmail flight that was of particular interest to me, and furthermore it gives me a chance to talk about stamp-collectors I knew, including a couple of Presidents. Doolittle, then a major in the Army Air Force, duplicated the route taken by Washington from New England, I believe, to Virginia. The pilot, of course, covered in a few hours the route that had taken Washington many days, and at each place where Washington had halted overnight he dropped a parachute bag of letters to be sent out from that post office. It was strictly a cover-collector's dream.

The reason I remember it was that a friend of mine, Philip R. Hough, superintendent of the Washington Birthplace National Monument, was an avid collector of covers and stamps issued in connection with the Washington anniversary, and wrote me a plaintive letter asking for help.

"Major Doolittle flew over here this morning and dropped a package of mail to go out from this post office," he said, "but of the thirty or forty letters there was none for this office"—that is, the National Monument. "I noticed one for the President, and suppose that they sent him others. If you have any duplicates, I sure would like to have the one from here."

It happened that Mr. Hoover was also very much interested in stamps and covers and had a fine collection, to which he was constantly adding. I was reluctant to ask him to break the set in order to provide one for Hough, but finally I did, and he very graciously agreed when he learned that Hough's collection was to be framed and left at the Monument as a permanent exhibit.

Mr. Hoover was the first real stamp-collector in the White House during my time. McKinley, T.R., Taft, Harding, Coolidge, and Wilson had no particular interest in the disposal of stamps and we handled them however we saw fit. Mr. Hoover, however, wanted a close watch kept for anything unusual to go into his collection, and later of course Franklin Roosevelt had a magnificent collection, which he vastly increased during his years in the White House.

F.D.R. probably knew more about stamp-collecting than any other President and enjoyed doing some of the work himself. The State Department and our office saved every foreign and commemorative stamp for him. Our system was to lay them aside in a safe place instead of sending them over to him as we received them. Then one day we knew we would get a call and Mr. Roosevelt would say, "Where are my stamps?" That meant he was going to take an evening off to work over his albums and relax with tweezers and microscopes.

He selected only such stamps as he decided would properly go into his collection, and always carefully returned the others for distribution elsewhere. His stamp collection was superior, I believe, even to his collection of ship models, which was of very great value.

Long before the Hoover and Roosevelt administrations, however, we had plenty of problems in connection with stamp-collectors. I supplied many covers and foreign stamps to private collectors at a time when the value of such collections was not generally recognized, and I have regretted many times that I did not take advantage of the opportunity to build up a collection of my own during the years when nobody cared what became of used stamps.

Eventually we developed a system for handling the stamps, because we realized that it was likely to become awkward if we supplied some private collectors and refused others. As a result we refused all private collectors—some of whom eventually offered considerable sums of money—and distributed stamps on a charitable basis as far as possible. During and since World War II there was and is an organization known as "Stamps for Veterans," which took stamps from our office and distributed them to veterans' hospitals where wounded men were encouraged to engage in this hobby as a part of curative therapy. Earlier, a similar scheme had been worked out in connection with the Civilian Conservation Corps camps, with the help of the Interior Department.

But in addition to these arrangements I always managed to keep a pretty fair collection of foreign and domestic stamps in my desk, and when kids wrote in to the President asking for stamps we were almost always able to send them something or other. Actually that was the way I would have liked to handle the whole stamp problem, but of course it wasn't practical—especially it wasn't practical if the President happened to have a collection himself.

Well, as things went along Mr. Hoover of course didn't have any time for stamp-collecting. He just kept working harder, and the state of the nation seemed to keep getting more and more uncomfortable. Or at least that's the way it seemed to me, because I had one of the most uncomfortable experiences of my career about that time—in the latter half of 1931, to be exact. For a while I thought it would mean the end of my White House career when and if the Democrats came into power.

The way it came about was this: Franklin Delano Roosevelt was emerging as a strong figure in the Democratic camp in the summer of 1931, and the Republicans had about decided he was the man they would have to beat if they were to stay in office. The political winds were blowing hard at the time, and one of the issues of which Mr. Roosevelt was trying to make political capital was a dispute over the proposed St. Lawrence River Seaway, in which Canada was just as much interested as the United States. As Governor of New York, which would be benefited by the seaway, Mr. Roosevelt wrote to President Hoover asking for information as to the status of negotiations with Canada. The fate of this letter at a time when political controversy was growing bitter throughout the country touched off a strange sequence of events of vital interest to me.

The villain in the case, from my viewpoint, was *Time* magazine, which on August 31, 1931, referred to the Roosevelt letter and said:

> When you write, address and mail a letter to President Herbert Hoover, The White House, Washington, D.C., it goes not to him, but to Ira Smith. Mr. Smith has a mustache. He sits at a big desk in the outer executive offices. . . . All day long he opens letters, scans them through gold-rimmed glasses. If your letter looks very important, he routes it to Private Secretary Theodore Joslin who may put it before the President. . . . [But] the chances are 1,000-to-1 against the President's ever seeing your letter at all. . . . Presumably the letter [from Mr. Roosevelt] went to Ira Smith and thereafter was reported "lost." . . . When it did finally turn up—with an answer—at the State Department, much explaining was necessary.

I read the article with surprise and consternation—surprise because I could not remember having seen the letter and consternation because it suggested that my office had been responsible for a blunder that would have very unfavorable political repercussions for the President. I made inquiries and discovered that my understudy, in my absence, had opened the letter from Governor Roosevelt, read it, and properly sent it to Mr. Hoover. The President directed that the letter be sent to the Secretary of State, with a request for information upon which to base a reply. When the letter reached the State Department, Acting Secretary William R. Castle was hurrying out of his office to catch a train for a short holiday at Hot Springs, Virginia. It is probable that he shoved the letter into his pocket, dashed away—and presumably forgot about it.

Castle, I suppose, discovered belatedly that the letter had not been answered. Just when this occurred I do not know, but the Acting Secretary was obviously in an awkward position. What to do? Castle had known Mr. Roosevelt for a long time, and he finally wrote him directly instead of returning the letter and the requested information to Mr. Hoover. This he did addressing the Governor as "Dear Frank," and stating that no negotiations were then in progress with Canada. The result was to make it appear, however erroneously, that Mr. Roosevelt had suffered an affront because his letter to the President had been answered by someone else.

Had *Time* magazine been correct in stating that the letter was reported "lost" after it came to me, my job would have ended right then. The President could not have excused me if I had carelessly sent such a letter to the State Department in the first place, and thus contributed to a situation that reacted unfavorably against Mr. Hoover. Nor would Mr. Roosevelt have forgotten it. The handling of the letter was an unhappy political blunder, but not on the part of the White House mail room.

As a matter of record, Mr. Roosevelt did not forget the

incident. When he moved into the White House after the election, one of his early questions was, "How about this man Ira Smith?" He first asked Admiral Cary Grayson, who expressed confidence in me. That did not entirely satisfy the President, however, and he later discussed my work with Col. Edmund Starling, head of the White House Secret Service. Starling reassured him, and Mr. Roosevelt finally dropped the matter when he had learned the full story.

When Mr. Hoover left the White House for good, we felt that we were witnessing the departure of an able and brilliant executive who had played into more hard luck than any President in many years. The personal files of the President, which were removed to his home at Palo Alto, contained a remarkable record of hard work and scientific planning that the public never heard much about. One reason they didn't hear about it was that a great hullabaloo was being raised about a coming attraction that was to turn the White House upside down for quite a few years. It was something called the New Deal.

# CHAPTER TEN

WHEN FRANKLIN DELANO ROOSEVELT BROUGHT THE NEW Deal into the White House during the great depression, it seemed as if everyone in the country was looking for a job except the new President and me. Both of us had our hands full, and then some.

During the last days of the Hoover administration the White House had been becalmed in a period of waiting, and my job of handling the President's mail had been comparatively routine, with only a few hundred letters a day coming in. With the arrival of F.D.R., we suddenly had action, new faces and Roosevelts all over the place, and so many tons of mail that, as I will explain later, we had to establish an entire new system for handling it.

Mr. Roosevelt always showed a keen interest in the mail and kept close watch on its trend. Nothing pleased him more than to know that I had to build up a big staff and often had to work until midnight to keep up with a run of 5000 to 8000 letters a day, and on some occasions many more thousands. He received regular reports on what was coming in, and frequently we sent him unusual letters, from which, with a fine knack for publicity, he would pick out material for newspaper stories.

Whenever there was a decrease in the influx of letters we could expect to hear from him or one of his secretaries, who wanted to know what was the matter—was the President losing his grip on the public? Everybody in the executive offices was keenly aware of the value of good public relations, and there was a lot of emphasis on proper handling of letters and of information for the newspapers.

Steve Early, the press secretary, was the sort of expert who could and did interrupt the President's talks with reporters to order, "Don't say that," or, "Don't answer that," and make it stick. But not everybody could be as experienced or as skillful in saying the right thing at the right time, and frequently we had some amusing complications because of the President's desire to show the greatest possible consideration to everyone who wrote to the White House in those troubled days.

On one occasion a cement worker in California wrote to Mr. Roosevelt and said that he had an exhibit of unusual craftsmanship which he wanted the President to see. Miss Margaret Le Hand, the President's personal secretary, wrote a pleasant letter in reply and told him that Mr. Roosevelt would be "interested in your exhibit."

Nobody gave it another thought until some weeks later, when a stranger came into the office and told me he had just arrived from California to erect an exhibit for the President. He said he had the exhibit outside, and where could he put it up? I went to the door and saw a huge truck pulled up at the curb.

"Just hold everything," I told him. I checked the correspondence, and talked to the man about the size of his exhibit. Then I advised Miss Le Hand that her invitation had been accepted, and where did she want the exhibit put? She finally arranged for him to use a hallway in the basement, and he began unloading large and complicated pieces of cement that looked like a cross between the Lincoln Memorial and a Coney Island roller-coaster.

He sweated and fussed around for a week, and finally put together a structure that was about eight feet by eight feet and reached almost to the ceiling. Apparently it was a castle in miniature. It had electric lights, music by radio, bells, chimes, and water that ran through the miniature rooms and into moats and over falls illuminated by colored lights. He had to use a network of hose and wires to get the thing into operation, and fuses were always blowing out or the water overflowed or something. The day he finally put it on display we went over to look, and it was fantastically unreal, with music playing, bells ringing, lights flashing, and water swirling all around.

Then it developed that the creator of this little number was in real life the builder of elaborate fishpools and similar decorative contrivances for gardens, and he wanted the President to endorse his creation, which he hoped to put on exhibition in various theaters. Mr. Roosevelt would not even go to look at it, and it was eventually carted back to California on a freight car—at quite an expense to the builder, but to the great relief of Miss Le Hand.

The cement castle seemed like quite a lot of excitement at

the time, but we soon learned to take such things in our stride as the New Dealers got down to business. There were Roosevelts and in-laws all over the landscape from then on. Nice, friendly people, too. Always something going on.

The thing that was going on most steadily was a stream of letters to F.D.R. demanding to know why in hell he didn't put his foot down and stop this habit his wife had of being constantly on the run somewhere or other and of always poking around in other people's business. I'm putting it mildly, of course, because the persons who wrote letters of that sort to the President were likely to use the most violent language.

I've heard various suggestions as to Mr. Roosevelt's reaction to these letters, and I feel sure that he valued his wife's firsthand knowledge of conditions. But it always seemed to me that Mrs. Roosevelt was going to lead her own life in her own way and there was not much the President or anyone else could say other than "What can *I* do about it?"

Mrs. Roosevelt got a huge mail, and there was much more approval of her actions than disapproval. She was always being asked for something or to do something or to intervene with the President. Many, many times she did pass along suggestions to various department heads and Cabinet members, and of course she helped a lot of people get jobs. After she started writing the newspaper column "My Day," her mail increased, and she had to build up a separate staff to handle it. Eventually, it included about a dozen girls and several men. I had to assign one of my clerks just to handle the letters that her staff referred to me concerning matters that were strictly the business of various departments, to which we forwarded them.

The real crisis came, however, over one of the most famous of the Roosevelt clan—the little black Scotty named Falla. We first saw Falla when Buzzie and Sistie Dall sometimes played up and down the halls with the dog in pursuit. They reminded me of the Teddy Roosevelt days, but not so noisy. There were stories about Falla in the newspapers, and soon letters began coming in for the dog. They were, I believe, the most sickening letters that ever got into the White House mail. Some woman with a dog would sit down and compose the *damnedest* pap as if her little doggie were writing to the President's little doggie, and it was enough to make you ill. When the Falla letters began arriving in large numbers, most of them "signed" with a dog's footprint, I rebelled. I sent all Falla correspondence over to Mrs. Roosevelt's social secretary, unopened.

"I'll take plenty," I said, "but I refuse to be a dog's secretary."

I didn't have anything against Falla, but the best dogs around the White House were the Roosevelts' Irish setters. They were beauties, and they sometimes liked to stretch out beside the President's desk, lying quietly but alert, when he had visitors. They were there during one little affair we attended in his office, and I spoke to Mr. Roosevelt about them merely because we didn't have anything else to talk about while waiting for the other guests to come in.

"Have those setters ever been hunted, Mr. President?" I asked.

I supposed he was going to say no, but Mrs. Roosevelt didn't give him a chance. She had overheard my question and obviously thought I was going to suggest something. She leaned over toward me and said, with considerable emphasis:

"No, and they're never going to be hunted either. They're household pets."

Mrs. Roosevelt was the most written-about and the most written-to First Lady, but she took it all in her stride, and I doubt that she ever lost her temper over anything critical that was ever said about her. She was too busy being herself.

Of all the new presidential aides, Louis Howe was probably the most unusual; certainly he was the strangest presidential secretary I ever knew. He was, of course, so ill that he would not last long, and he seemed to realize it. A slight, thin-faced man, he never wasted a word or a motion. He obviously tried to conserve his waning strength and never lifted a hand around the office if he could avoid it. He didn't even sign all his own letters. He mostly seemed to just sit and watch and listen, and I suppose he was Mr. Roosevelt's most valuable adviser. Without seeming to do anything, Howe kept close track of everything that went on. Even our mental attitudes. Once his secretary wandered into my office, possibly on Howe's instructions, and in the course of a chat asked me what I really thought of the President.

Now I considered Mr. Roosevelt one of the most remarkable men I had ever seen operating at close range, and all of us were glad to see that at last we were getting some action around the White House. But her question obviously was a bit more personal. My impression at that time was that the President was always playing his part like a good actor. He was jovial, chatty, and informal, and this struck me as an almost professional attitude of good-fellowship. He could turn on his dazzling smile as if somebody had pressed a button and sent a brilliant beam from a lighthouse out across the sea—shining on whatever ship happened to be there. I never felt, as I suppose most people did, that there was anything particularly personal about his manner toward me. And why should there have been?

So I merely said, "The President seems to be the most politic man I ever saw."

She looked at me in amazement and then bristled with indignation. She stoutly denied that my observation was even partly correct. She obviously felt that whenever Mr. Roosevelt gave her a pleasant look it was something very specially reserved for her, and I think the President had the ability to make that impression on most persons, both great and small. I don't mean that his friendliness was insincere. I mean it was just a charming, almost irresistible knack that he used, perhaps, subconsciously.

He could even do it over the radio, much to my distress. When he advised millions of listeners in one of his fireside chats to "tell me your troubles," most of them believed implicitly that he was speaking to them personally and immediately wrote him a letter. It was months before we managed to swim out of *that* flood of mail.

The President's most prolific correspondents, strangely enough, were two well-known characters who also called on him regularly—Secretary of Interior Harold Ickes and Secretary of Agriculture Henry Wallace. Both of them wrote to Mr. Roosevelt frequently and lengthily. In fact, at one time it got so we could expect a letter from Ickes on some subject or other almost every day at three o'clock in the afternoon—presumably after he had wrestled with an idea at the luncheon table and then had time to get it down on paper.

Ickes always impressed me as an outstanding Secretary of Interior, but he couldn't possibly mind his own business. His letters covered a wide field of subjects, and were especially frequent during the period when Mr. Roosevelt was pushing the Supreme Court "packing" bill. Wallace's letters did not cover so wide a range, but had little to do with his own department. He wanted to run the State Department by giving advice directly to the President on how to handle foreign affairs.

Of all the Roosevelt advisers, I suppose the most disliked was Harry Hopkins. I didn't care much for him myself, but I developed a sort of grudging admiration for the way he operated. He gave the impression of being sloppy, lazy, indifferent, and sometimes ruthless. That impression was not very accurate. Like Louis Howe, he was desperately ill and needed to conserve his strength. He would listen to a long discussion of some problem without saying a word or giving any sign of interest. Then he would settle the matter with perhaps one sentence or merely a nod in answer to a question. Usually settled it for good, too.

Another person who made his appearance around the White House during the Roosevelt days was George Allen, whom F.D.R. made a Commissioner for the District of Columbia. One day Allen passed word along that the President had agreed to permit use of his name by the National Foundation for Infantile Paralysis, of which Basil O'Connor was head. He said a little stunt had been arranged to raise money for the Foundation in connection with the President's birthday, and that it was being suggested on two radio shows —Eddie Cantor and the Lone Ranger—that people send dimes for the Foundation to the White House as contributions.

"It's all very unofficial, of course, but keep your eyes open," Allen said. "You may get a trickle of dimes in the mail."

It was a remark I'll never forget. Both Cantor and the Lone Ranger did talk about the campaign on their shows, and the Lone Ranger urged kids to send a dime each to the President for use in fighting infantile paralysis. Two days later the roof fell in—on me. We had been handling about 5000 letters a day at that time. We got 30,000 on the day the March of Dimes began producing. We got 50,000 the next day. We got 150,000 the third day. We kept on getting incredible numbers, and the Government of the United States darned near stopped functioning because we couldn't clear away enough dimes to find the official White House mail.

I screamed for help as soon as my staff could get the bags full of dimes piled up enough to let me get out of the office. We got fifty extra postal clerks, but we still couldn't find anything but scrawled and finger-marked envelopes from every kid who could get his hands on a dime. Picking out the President's official mail was like looking for a needle in a haystack. Replies to invitations that Mrs. Roosevelt had sent out for a formal dinner were buried under tens of thousands of letters from all over the United States and Canada. She didn't get them until two weeks after the dinner.

We began sending bags of mail to the offices of the various presidential secretaries, and they dug into them in searcrh for important letters they were expecting. Judge Rosenman abandoned writing the President's speeches and began sorting mail. Mrs. James Roosevelt volunteered to help. The stenographers and anybody else available spent all their spare time fumbling through huge stacks of letters, many of the staff voluntarily working hours of overtime without pay. The offices, desks, and corridors were stacked with mail sacks, and we had to put police on special duty each night when we finally closed up and went wearily home.

It was days before we began to restore some kind of routine and it was four months before we had cleaned up the debris. Being completely inexperienced in such enterprises, we had to devise a special set-up to handle the 2,680,000 dimes that rolled in during the campaign.

The first wave of response in 1938 was largely from children, because the Lone Ranger had emphasized the idea of putting a dime in an envelope and sending it to the President. Every time we emptied a mailbag $8 or $10 worth of loose coins that had cut through the envelopes would fall out. Then, as the idea grew, dimes were sent in all sorts of ways that caused additional work. I developed a deep bitterness toward persons who used scotch tape to stick coins on a card. Every dime we received that way had to be washed in a special solution—we finally found fire-extinguisher fluid was best—before the Treasury would accept it. Once we got 100 yards of dimes in scotch tape.

Other dimes were received in a wax design the size of a football. We had to boil it down. Thousands were baked into birthday cakes. Once we had to break up a concrete brick loaded with coins. A woman who wanted to contribute but had no money had her hair cut off and sent it in with the suggestion that we sell it. It brought eighty dimes. We received an aluminum cane made of hollow tubing into which were jammed 650 dimes. A gallon can containing $300 arrived from a bomber squadron.

One donor punched a hole in a dime (making it worthless) and tied it with twine to a huge cardboard tag labeled "The White House." I sent it around for Mr. Roosevelt to see. He kept the dime and returned the card with a new dime to go in the collection and a note saying, "I hope you have a good dime." One of the clerks kept the President's dime to give to his grandchild as a memento, putting another in its place. I didn't tell him that, as usual, Mr. Roosevelt had no money in his pocket and that his secretary had furnished the memento coin.

During the big rush of dime mail one of our biggest jobs was just counting the money, but later we merely weighed it after separating the silver from the checks and currency. Then I would send it over to the Treasury in an armored car with two Secret Service men carrying tommy guns and they would give me currency to turn over to the Foundation. Later we got an army truck with a guard to deliver the silver. The campaign grew in later years and we received more than

$1,500,000 in 1945, when there were larger contributions and not so many letters as in the first year.

People still kept thinking up spectacular ways to deliver dimes, however. In one publicity stunt, 600,000 dimes were sent under guard from Los Angeles, where they had been contributed by listeners to a radio breakfast program. The trip cost $670, whereas a check could have been mailed for 3 cents. Upon arrival, the people in charge wanted to present the coins personally to Mr. Roosevelt. Part of the silver was put on the elevator, but the load was too much and it wouldn't move. The publicity stunt was a bit overloaded, too, and ended at that point.

After the first year, we made special preparations for the March of Dimes, taking on extra clerks in January and keeping them until we cleaned up the work in March, but I never saw George Allen after that without a shudder. A "trickle of dimes," indeed!

After Mr. Roosevelt had the executive offices rebuilt to provide more room there was a basement under all of the structure except the Cabinet room and a part of the President's office. The rest of his office was directly over a storeroom which divided in the middle by a wire partition, thus forming a cage where we put many of the thousands of odd gifts that came to the White House. A ventilator leading to the President's office was inside the wire cage, which was securely locked.

One day the Secret Service men came to me and said they were worried about the ventilator, which opened outside the building. It might, they said, occur to some crank to plant a bomb in the ventilator, since it was under the President's desk. They said it had been decided to make some structural changes to eliminate the possibility. They took a key to the cage and in the next day or so workmen arrived and began making changes. The next time I went into the cage I took a look at what they had done. A wooden partition about five feet by four had been constructed from floor to ceiling. It had a door that was securely padlocked. I was curious about it, because it was the strangest bomb-prevention device I could imagine.

One of the President's most skillful stenographers did his work in the basement offices near my desk and had a key to the wire cage. I noticed that he frequently went to the cage, and one day when I was there he came out of the little room. The door was open and I saw a small desk and a chair inside. I nodded to the stenographer.

"Oh," I said, "got a machine in there, eh?"

He laughed. "I was just getting some reports from upstairs," he said.

I didn't say anything more, but I noticed that the stenographer frequently went to the little room, where he obviously took down whatever conversation went on in the President's office. We never discussed it, and I guess my staff kept on believing the Secret Service story about bomb prevention.

Contacts around the White House were free and easy during the New Deal, and the Roosevelts were always thoughtful of the staff. The President received hundreds of birthday cakes each year, and he would pick out one of the grandest and invite everybody in for tea. Mrs. Roosevelt usually came too, and sometimes brought her own guests. The President seemed to enjoy these breaks in the routine more than anyone else, and he made everybody feel at home.

On one occasion when the cake was brought in he remarked that it was a particularly handsome one. On the top was a coach with six horses molded in spun sugar. Then, with a twinkle in his eye, the President turned to Gus Gennerich, a Secret Service man, and said in a commanding voice:

"Gus, bring me George Washington's sword that I may cut this cake!"

Everybody loved it, and the girls all gasped, but when it came to cutting the fruit cake the President used an ordinary knife. Most of the girls on the staff secretly wrapped their slices of cake in their handkerchiefs to take home as souvenirs. I ate mine. It was very tasty.

There was always about Mr. Roosevelt a kind of infectious confidence and buoyancy that was felt by those who worked with him, and even by those who saw him only occasionally. But during the terrible years of World War II there was a drastic change both in the President and in the atmosphere around the White House. Mr. Roosevelt soon became absorbed in the long-range war and postwar problems, and gave less and less attention to immediate political and governmental questions at home. Matters that he would have handled personally during his first two terms were frequently delegated to subordinates, and this led to blunders, quarrels, and misunderstandings. Many letters, particularly from members of Congress, came to the White House in those days complaining that affairs of political importance were being neglected or were being bungled—in strange contrast to the White House operations before the war.

It has always seemed to me that Mr. Roosevelt's withdrawal from such matters in order to devote himself to the war problems may have opened the way for later charges that Communist-minded persons had infiltrated into government positions. The President was too astute a politican in normal times to fail to foresee and halt conditions that later gave rise to Congressional investigation of alleged Communist spying. But in the war days Mr. Roosevelt was preoccupied, and inclined to shove such matters aside in favor of grandiose global planning.

This was true before we actually got into the war, but when Pearl Harbor came, the trend was drastically intensified. There was also a sudden change in all White House affairs. A bomb shelter was built underground at the east end of the White House and everybody got a gas mask. We were lectured by Army officers and had regular air-raid drills. Everybody had to keep his gas mask on his desk, and every so often the fire gongs would ring the air-raid alarm and we would assemble in specified offices for drill. My office was one of the assembly points and I was in charge there, which meant that I had a gas mask I could talk through. Nobody else could talk through his gas mask. It was rather pleasant on those occasions.

Soldiers were moved into the barracks south of the old State Department Building and a guard line was established around the White House. At intervals a patrol, fully armed, would march around the yard changing the guard, which was maintained day and night.

The wartime secrecy and precautions for protection of the President added considerably to our work, especially since many new figures, both military and civilian, were suddenly thrust to the foreground of governmental affairs. A good number of them had strange ideas about what should be "top secret" or "for the eyes of the President only." This was especially true of the State Department, which was overrun with young squirts who thought that anything that passed through their hands or was received in code was too secret for anyone but the Chief Executive to see. It took us quite a while to convince them that it would be all right for us to handle translations of birthday messages and similar communications from foreign dignitaries, even in wartime.

Every White House employee was checked by the Secret Service or the Federal Bureau of Investigation, and if there was the slightest suspicion of any person, that person was removed or transferred. We had one girl of foreign descent in our office who caused some concern. One day the Secret Service came around and asked me to hold out any mail she received at the office.

"There's something funny going on," I was told. "This girl has been using White House stationery to write to a fellow in New York who has connections with the I. G. Farben outfit in Germany."

I don't know what else the Secret Service did in investigating that case, but they certainly watched her mail. They even went through the wastebasket by her desk every evening after she left the office, and that is where they finally struck pay dirt. One evening they found the wastebasket full of half-written letters to the man, all of them crumpled up into balls. When they were smoothed out and read it was obvious that she had been having a quarrel with the New Yorker, and just as obvious that she was trying to compose a love letter that would patch things up. Either that, or she was using an interesting code language. As far as I know, the only thing the Secret Service discovered was an unsuspected love affair. But just to be on the safe side the girl was transferred anyway—without ever knowing that she had been the object of investigation.

The tenor of mail to the President changed, too, after Pearl Harbor. I recall that before we got into World War I many pro-German letters came to the White House. There were pro-Germans on the White House staff at that time, too, and they didn't hesitate to express their opinions, because most Americans considered the European struggle begun in 1914 to be of no concern to us as a nation. But World War II found Mr. Roosevelt strongly opposed to the Axis from the beginning, and this position was reflected in the mail. There were many protests against war in general, but letters favoring the Axis were few and far between, while large numbers of persons wrote in to praise the President or to urge that he take a still stronger stand.

After Pearl Harbor, there was a flood of letters and telegrams urging the President not to "get excited" and not to "rush headlong into war," but by the time these arrived we were already at war and the mail room was overburdened with angry letters demanding elimination of the Japanese and offering the writers' services in the war effort. At this time somebody spread the idea that the Government needed fine human hair in the manufacture of precision instruments such as bombsights, and we received contributions enough to make a rope stretching from Washington to Berlin. We sent them over to the Bureau of Standards, which probably dumped them in the wastebasket. Large sums of money also were sent in, usually in very small amounts, with letters urging the Government to use the money for bullets to be fired in the war against the Japanese. All such funds were turned over to the Treasury.

The strain on the President and those close to him sometimes seemed almost unbearable in the early days of the war, but Mr. Roosevelt stood up under it better than almost anyone else. We saw him less often because of the tight wartime regulations and the pressure of his work, but during the first year he merely seemed a bit older and, naturally, less jovial. But after that it began to be apparent that his condition was deteriorating, and there was a good deal of concern about his health before the 1944 election campaign when he began to suffer from periodic colds and failed to bounce back as rapidly as in the past.

People began writing in to ask about his condition, but the official position of the White House was always reassuring, as perhaps it should be in such circumstances. I would not, of course, pretend to any knowledge of medicine, but strictly from the viewpoint of a layman who occasionally saw the President it seemed to me that Mr. Roosevelt's health was far from robust.

There was, naturally, an inclination to be reassuring and

to avoid causing alarm. Furthermore, the state of the President's health was of tremendous importance in international affairs at a critical point in world history. These things obviously entered into the reassuring White House and other authoritative statements, but we of the staff knew the President was not his old self.

In January, at the beginning of F.D.R.'s fourth term, my wife and I received a note from Presidential Secretary Early inviting us to attend a Service of Intercession on the twentieth. We arrived at the White House that Saturday just as General of the Army George C. Marshall and his wife went in, and we were all taken immediately to the East Room, where rows of chairs had been arranged in a semicircle. The ladies of the Roosevelt family sat together just in front of us, each of them carrying a bouquet of violets. Mrs. Roosevelt's was enormous and the perfume was strong in the room. The choir from St. John's Church was massed near the big windows, where their robes made a warm spot of color among the display of flags.

The President sat in the center of the front row and beside him or behind him were the great names of his administration—the great names of a bitter war that was just turning toward a day when victory could no longer be denied. It was a friendly gathering, yet solemn and full of portent, as if these men realized that the tragic years of war now nearing an end were only the beginning of the test our country must face. Mr. Roosevelt must have thought, too, of his impending journey to the Yalta Conference.

The choir sang "O God, our help in ages past . . . be

Thou our guide," and there were prayers for the President of the United States and for our country and for our enemies and for victory.

When the services ended, we stood very silent for a moment and then for a few moments more as we waited for the President to depart. But he made no move. His wheel chair was brought in by an attendant but, almost impatiently, he motioned it away. Everyone watched and waited, and still the President remained in his chair. His daughter Anna turned to face us and smiled. With a little shrug she seemed to say, "Well, he has something on his mind."

Finally, without a word, Mr. Roosevelt turned as if he had awakened from a deep reverie and beckoned to us. We all seemed to understand what he wanted and we formed a line that filed past him so that he could shake hands with each one. When I stepped close to him I was shocked to see how tired and ill he looked, how gray and old and thin he had become. He didn't say anything. Just shook hands.

The death of Mr. Roosevelt at Warm Springs, however, was a shock to all of us. I had been inclined to draw a comparison with the illness of Woodrow Wilson and to fear that the President's health would continue to decline gradually. The news flash from Warm Springs therefore was as much a surprise to us as to the rest of the world. For weeks after Mr. Roosevelt died we received letters demanding an investigation of his death and suggesting that there had been foul play, but of course none of them was based on any knowledge of the facts.

After the funeral, Mrs. Roosevelt asked all the staff to

come around on April 20 to say good-by. Mrs. Boettiger, James Roosevelt and his wife, and Faye Emerson Roosevelt were with her. When we returned to our desks, each of us found there one of the countless little trinkets with which the President had always littered his own desk. Mrs. Roosevelt had sent them around as mementos. Mine was a little gray donkey.

# CHAPTER ELEVEN

A GREAT MANY WOMEN AS WELL AS MEN, I IMAGINE, HAVE dreamed and schemed of how to get to live in the White House, and some of them have been unpleasantly surprised and disappointed when they made the grade. The disappointment was political or social in some instances, but most First Ladies have suffered varying degrees of unhappiness about the deplorable condition of the White House and their inability to get anything done about it.

It's an uncomfortable old mansion. It always needs repairs. It was once infested with rats, some rooms were so damp that the paper peeled, it had an antique heating system, and when the Harry Trumans moved in it was clear that something had to be done or one of these days the roof would fall in. No wonder new occupants were often surprised and disappointed.

It remained, however, for the Harry Trumans to reverse the procedure of the past. They were not eager in the beginning to take up residence in the White House, and Mrs. Bess Truman especially was not highly excited by the prospect of social or political goings-on. They felt they had been thrust by fate into the old mansion, and they seemed to expect the worst. Naturally, it wasn't as bad as all that. But the interesting thing to me was that it was the Trumans who finally did something about the White House. That was, in its own way, quite an achievement for any President.

The condition of the presidential mansion as I have indicated before, was a disgrace to the nation when I first went to Washington during the McKinley administration, and despite various changes and repairs, it remained in a more or less disgraceful state right up to the time I retired in 1948. At the turn of the century, the walls of the place were constantly damp, the floors were warped, and the stairs were creaky and rickety. I remember once when one of the famous billiard champions of the day was invited to give an exhibition at the White House. He arrived eager and willing, but the table in the billiard room had been so nearly ruined by dampness that he could scarcely drive a ball around it. He soon gave up the attempt.

The mansion was not called the White House officially in those days, but was known as the Executive Mansion, because it contained the crowded presidential offices as well as the living quarters of the President's family. It was adjacent to low swampy ground that ran down to the Potomac, and a rainy spell would bring water up as high as what is now Constitution Avenue. The mosquitoes flourished in the standing water along the flats between the mansion and the river, and the neighborhood was so unhealthy that White House grounds police had to be shifted at regular intervals because so many developed malaria. The President, however, didn't have anybody to shift with.

A few changes in the White House and the grounds are naturally made with every administration, but in McKinley's time all efforts to get Congress to appropriate needed funds for repairs were futile, and almost nothing was done. The only changes I recall were the removal of the sentry box that had stood on the grounds since the Civil War, when it was built to shelter guards on cold nights, and the filling in of a cistern that Mrs. Rutherford Hayes had had built on the southeast corner of the White House. The cistern had an engine to pump drinking water to the private apartments upstairs, and was considered quite a fancy addition to the place during the Hayes administration.

But even if the McKinleys couldn't get anything done, they got a great many suggestions for tearing down the mansion and building a new one on higher ground. Mrs. Mary Foote Henderson, whose husband had been a Senator, carried on quite a vigorous campaign in 1898 for a new mansion on Meridian Hill, where it was proposed to develop large terraces and gardens that would overlook the city. There were a lot of suggestions for other sites then and later, but they never got anywhere, and I guess George Washington's original choice of a building lot wasn't so bad after all, because none of the tenants I knew ever threatened to break the lease on 1600 Pennsylvania Avenue.

Teddy Roosevelt got something done when he became President, including the building of the executive-offices wing, but he came in for a lot of criticism by newspapers that regarded the changes as contrary to the original architectural conception. The *Washington Post* described the wing as "a wart on the White House," and various political foes of the

President took up the criticism in Congress and elsewhere. T.R., however, had studied the old plans of the mansion, and the repairs and changes that were undertaken then were in line with the original plans. He went right ahead without paying much attention to his critics. The greenhouse was eliminated and became a passageway to the offices. The old glass partition in the main lobby of the mansion was taken away, and the old staircases were removed to make way for a grand staircase at the east end of the corridor. These changes made the place look better, but they did nothing much about the roof or the floor supports in the living quarters, which were to become a problem later.

There was a lot of mail at the time in favor of or opposing the changes in the mansion, and I was amazed by the interest people everywhere took in the preservation of historic buildings. For the most part, the writers were perfectly willing for the presidential family to be as comfortable as possible, but not at the sacrifice of a national shrine.

The rumpus quieted down by the time Mr. Taft was President, and he had no trouble in getting authorization to double the size of the executive offices to take care of our greatly expanded staff. There were some roof and attic repairs made during the Coolidge administration, but on Christmas Eve of 1929, during Mr. Hoover's term, fire gutted the interior of the offices and did great damage. We were in a state of confusion for months after that, and for a while my desk was a billiard table in the basement of the mansion.

The offices were remodeled by F.D.R. and the working space about tripled. A new kitchen, a carpenter shop, and storage vaults under the north porch and the roadway were installed, and the east-wing offices were added for police, protective research for the Secret Service, and Mrs. Roosevelt's correspondence section.

Mr. Truman wanted to do some additional construction, including an auditorium and a cafeteria, on the west end of the executive office, as well as offices for various administrative assistants, but somebody talked about it carelessly to the reporters and the old cry of "destroying" the historic White House was raised again. It was a pretty vicious campaign while it lasted, with the Washington newspapers for the most part attacking the plans.

Mr. Truman already had the reluctant approval of the Fine Arts Commission and an appropriation from Congress, but so much fuss was raised that Congress finally revoked the appropriation, although work had already started. The result was a lot of confusion around the executive offices and a lot more inconvenience, but the thing that I rather liked was that the President didn't let his critics get him down. He came right back with plans for the famous balcony on the White House itself, and put it through in the face of the most bitter opposition from experts who accused him of making a farce of the original architectural plans.

Not many persons realize how keen a student of history Mr. Truman has been for many years, and in this instance he demonstrated that he knew more about the original plans than the experts did. He produced evidence that the original drawing for the mansion provided for just the sort of balcony he had built, but his evidence didn't come out until after the big newspaper rumpus over the Truman porch had died down, and so, few people realized that the President was an easy winner in the argument. To say nothing of getting a place where he can take his ease after a hard day's work running the country.

After Mr. Truman had finally forced the issue on White House repairs and Congress was ready to spend $1,000,000 fixing things up, the real story began to come out. Engineers discovered that it was a miracle that the place hadn't fallen down long ago. The structural deficiencies were so great that they would have caused any other building to have been condemned as a menace. Only a two-inch beam kept the President's private bathroom from tumbling into the basement. For years, the experts discovered, the most famous figures in the nation and in the world had been standing frequently under the heavy ornamental ceiling of the famous East Room, which was likely to fall at any time. It had been completely loosened from the beams and was held up only by nails. Well, after having spent many thousands of hours in the place during the last half century, I was happy to take my hat off to Mr. Truman for getting something done about it.

The President gave an impression of wanting to get things done from the first day that he came to the White House, although he certainly was far from confident. He asked the staff into his office, and it was a shock after so many years of F.D.R., to see the place denuded of its ship models, flags, trophies, and trinkets. Mr. Truman was pleasant and businesslike, and urged us to do as well for him as we had for Mr. Roosevelt.

There was a change, however, in the atmosphere around the White House. Mr. Truman's self-styled chief secretary, Ed McKim, seemed constantly to be worrying about whether the staff was capable of "keeping things confidential"—something we had been doing satisfactorily for a good many years. McKim brought in a couple of special investigators who had worked for the Truman Committee in the Senate and had them check on whether the White House office set-up was airtight. Nothing happened on whatever they may have reported, but McKim moved on to another job after a short time.

Before he went, however, I showed him how the mail room operated one day, and later he visited the special staff that had handled Mrs. Roosevelt's mail.

"So this is 'My Day,' eh?" McKim remarked sardonically, in reference to Mrs. Roosevelt's newspaper column. "Well, that day is gone."

He fired the whole staff and abolished the separate office that had been sat up to assist Mrs. Roosevelt. It didn't stick, however. Mrs. Truman heard about it and went to the President. Part of the staff was hired back and kept on handling Mrs. Truman's mail, which ran quite heavy at the time.

We appreciated Mrs. Truman's attitude and, in an unusual way, we had a chance later to do something for her. She came to me one day not long before the President's birthday and said that there was nothing that gave Mr. Truman more pleasure than opening his own presents. She understood that the Secret Service detail had a rule that all packages had to be inspected before they were delivered to the President, but she wondered whether, in this case, there was some way . . . I said I thought we might find some way, but I couldn't promise anything.

There are a number of rules to be observed in handling the White House mail, especially packages, as will be explained later. In this case we interpreted the regulations loosely. Among the gifts arriving were many neckties sent in honor of the former haberdasher of Independence, Missouri. We put them under the fluoroscope and okayed them without opening the packages. There were other parcels of which we were doubtful, but most of them we were able to open and reseal so that they did not appear to have been tampered with. We turned over to Mrs. Truman quite a batch of birthday presents that appeared to be fresh from the mail truck. I don't believe the President ever caught on. He tore off the wrappers with enthusiasm, and had a big time that day.

People everywhere seemed to want to send Mr. Truman some token of goodwill when he became President. There are always many gifts coming to the White House, some of them from persons who are trying to advertise some article they have for sale and some of them in the category of freak gifts. In the case of Mr. Truman I have a list of gifts received that provides an interesting catalogue of the peculiar packages mailed to a President. It follows:

| | |
|---|---|
| Kansas City, Mo. | 3 sport shirts |
| Honolulu, Hawaii | Gavel made of teakwood taken from the damaged deck of the U.S.S. *Missouri* |

| | |
|---|---|
| New York, N.Y. | Miniature good-luck charm of the "Surrender Spot" aboard the U.S.S. *Missouri* |
| Philadelphia, Pa. | 7 pairs of ladies' nylon hose |
| Cascapedia, P.Q., Canada | 41-lb. salmon |
| New Orleans, La. | Genuine panama hat |
| Rapid City, S.D. | 1 worn white shirt |
| Waterford, Erie, Pa. | Old $5 bill printed in 1775 |
| Toledo, Ohio | Model of "Jeep Fire Engine" |
| Portland, Ore. | 3 Spanish onions |
| St. Louis, Mo. | Pair of satin pajamas |
| Ilion, N.Y. | Baby's diaper |
| Hope, Ark. | Watermelon weighing 140 lbs. |
| Menasha, Wis. | Fishing tackle |
| Sioux City, Iowa | "Victory Apple" with a natural "V" on its skin |
| St. Paul, Minn. | Lawn mower |
| Lillington, N.C. | Yam weighing 6½ lbs. |
| Duluth, Minn. | Professional horseshoes |
| Dumbarton Center, N.H. | Metal Weeder |
| Centerville, Tenn. | A small potato that had attached itself to an old rusty hinge through natural growth |
| Detroit, Mich. | Doll (14″ tall) made to the likeness of President Truman |
| San Diego, Calif. | Toy airplane |
| Dallas, Tex. | Walking cane |
| San Francisco, Calif. | Caricature sketch of President Truman |
| San Francisco, Calif. | 6 bow ties |
| Long Island City, N.Y. | Gold-finished toilet seat |
| Durham, N.C. | Basket carved from a peach stone |
| Trinidad, B.W.I. | Live parrot |
| Nacona, Tex. | Pair of leather boots |
| Kansas City, Kan. | Rabbit foot |
| Pittsburgh, Pa. | Hand-knitted American flag |
| New Hampton, N.Y. | Miniature plastic piano |

| | |
|---|---|
| Bronxville, N.Y. | Small toy donkey made of wool |
| New York, N.Y. | 2 frozen pheasants |
| Port Huron, Mich. | Rag rug |
| New York, N.Y. | Nazi flag |
| Brooklyn, N.Y. | Embroidered picture of President Truman |
| Highland Park, Mich. | Floor lamp |
| South Bend, Ind. | Pair of miniature boxing gloves |
| Waterloo, Iowa | Live turkey weighing 40 lbs. |
| Philadelphia, Pa. | 3 Missouri mule shoes |
| Phoenix, Ariz. | Pair of "Antsy Pants" shorts |
| Centralia, Wash. | Small hand-carved jackass |
| Brooklyn, N.Y. | Ukulele with instruction book on how to play |
| St. Petersburg, Fla. | Polished "swordfish snout" to be used as paper-cutter |
| Tuckahoe, N.Y. | Hand-painted eggshell made in the form of a vase |
| Lake Geneva, Wis. | Box of assorted cheese |
| Chicago, Ill. | 11 comic books |
| Washington, D.C. | Caviar |
| Baltimore, Md. | Ice-cream telegram |
| Kansas City, Mo. | Four-leaf clover |
| Los Angeles, Calif. | "Ant Village" (containing live ants) |
| Wyoming, Ill. | Old baby shoe |
| Kansas City, Mo. | Bugle used when President was in Battery D, World War I |
| Kankakee, Ill. | Small model of dog hand carved from a cake of soap |
| Guiuan, Samar, P.I. | Japanese Army fighting flag |
| Spokane, Wash. | Rainbow trout weighing 23½ lbs. when cleaned |
| New York, N.Y. | Case of hair tonic |
| Mitchell, S.D. | Corsage and pair of earrings (both made from pheasant feathers) |
| Erie, Pa. | Cherry pie weighing 44 lbs. |

| | |
|---|---|
| San Antonio, Tex. | Miniature saddle |
| Brecksville, Ohio | Fly swatter |
| Greenwood, Miss. | Garbage can |
| Kansas City, Kan. | Small model of an old-fashioned plow |
| Milwaukee, Wis. | Hand-made Indian rug |
| Kent, Ohio | Hand-painted Easter egg |
| Curwensville, Pa. | Two white kittens |
| Yakima, Wash. | Knitted woolen "jester's" cap |
| Paris, France | 2 loaves of French bread |
| Aguadilla, P.R. | 3 pairs of lady's gloves |
| New York, N.Y. | Game of chess |
| Athens, Greece | Cigarettes, olives, and olive oil |

It was quite a while before things began to get back to normal under the Trumans. For some reason or other, Grace Tully, who had been F.D.R.'s personal secretary, was kept sitting in idleness around the office for weeks. She finally departed after she had arranged to take along Mr. Roosevelt's records for classification and deposit in the archives.

General Vaughan, the President's military aide, and Commodore Vardaman, the naval aide, came up one day with the idea that they would handle all the President's contacts with veterans, presumably on the theory that there was political gold in them hills. Among other things, they ordered that all mail from veterans and servicemen be turned over to them instead of being forwarded to the various departments for answer.

This gave me the only chuckle I had in several weeks. At that time we were getting letters from veterans and servicemen who wanted to know what had happened to their insurance, when they would get a bonus, when was their discharge coming through, where could they get jobs, why couldn't they get a house to live in, and where in hell was the postwar world they had been told about? The next morning I carefully laid out 600 such love notes from soldiers and veterans and sent them around to General Vaughan. He took one look and asked:

"How long have these been accumulating?"

"That's just the morning mail," he was told.

I must say the General reacted rapidly. "Take 'em away," he ordered and that was the end of his handling the veterans' mail. Commodore Vardaman heard about Vaughan's experience and canceled his order for the mail from Navy veterans before he even got the first batch.

On another occasion Vaughan brought around a friend of his who was representative of a soft-drink company. He told John Boardley, a Negro messenger, that a soft drink vending machine was being installed in the office and that Boardley was personally to handle it, collect the money, and make regular accountings.

"General," Boardley said, "I can't do that. I've got too much to do."

"You'll do what I tell you," the General replied.

Boardley went immediately to the executive clerk and submitted his formal request for retirement, to which he was then entitled. The executive clerk smoothed things over by letting Boardley delegate the handling of the soft-drink machine to another messenger.

The only time I ever had any trouble with the Secret Service was after Mr. Truman made George Drescher, who had been his guard when he was Vice-President, the head of the White House detail. George was a jolly big fellow who had always been easy to get along with. About this time, however, I had arranged to remodel a garage in order to use it as a receiving room for the mail department, and I had the approval of Howard Crim, who was in charge of White House buildings. Drescher apparently did not get along with Crim, and he vetoed the plan, which had to be approved by the Secret Service. I asked him way.

"Well," he said, "there might sometime be riots around here and we would want to use that garage as a place in which to conceal soldiers."

This seemed to me to make very little sense, but we probably never would have got the idea okayed by the Secret Service if George had remained in that job. Before he left, however, an amusing little thing happened.

On one occasion when Mrs. Truman was in Missouri, the President sent around word that we were all invited to an affair in the East Room. The Broadway comedians Olsen and Johnson were the principal stars, and they went through their zany stunts with enthusiasm, but failed in their efforts to get Mr. Truman to play the piano. It was an uproarious occasion, and it was the first time I had been in the East Room since we attended the intercession service at which Mr. Roosevelt was present.

As we left, my wife went out first. I noticed Drescher, big and broad, standing just outside the door, but nobody else seemed to be around to say good-by. I had just said, "Hiyah, George," when I saw a hand reach out from behind him to catch the arm of my wife, who was heading on down the hall. She stopped and peered and then blushed. By the time I was up even with George, she was shaking hands with Mr. Truman. He had been completely concealed behind his huge Secret Service man.

The Trumans were very folksy, although apparently somewhat uncomfortable, when they first moved into the White House. They found that living at 1600 Pennsylvania Avenue wasn't the same as living at home. Mr. Truman fretted under the weight of his new burdens, and it took him quite a while to decide he liked being President. He kept close track of how the mail was running. It was pretty high at first, but he was especially interested in whether it ran as high as Mr. Roosevelt's average. I always had to say that it didn't.

# CHAPTER TWELVE

SOMEWHERE IN THE UNITED STATES RIGHT AT THIS MINUTE several persons are exercising their inalienable right to sit down and knock off a letter to the President. One of them may be an indignant housewife complaining about prices at the butcher shop or the quality of teen-age entertainment on the radio. Another may be a big businessman expressing his views on taxation. Still another may be suggesting that the President try Aunt Martha's home remedy for his cold.

Several thousand persons write to the Chief Executive every day on every subject you can think of and a great many that you could never imagine. Some are serious thinkers, some are busybodies, and some are just crazy, like the man who asked for "a list of all the misses in the U.S. so I can solve the mystery of who is Miss Hush on the radio."

Most of the people who write to the President expect him to read and answer their letters, or to perform some small favor such as putting them in touch with a soldier in Munich, selling a fancy piece of embroidery, addressing the graduating class at Northside High School, or dropping an atom bomb on some foreign capital. Some of them suspect that their letters might not reach the President, and they include a bitter denunciation of nosy secretaries and clerks who ought to be put in jail if they open letters addressed to someone else. Some of these unusual notations on envelopes addressed to the President were: "Mrs. Rosenfelt, kindly give this to your husband, thank you." "This letter must not be opened by anyone but the Pres. Give it to him when he starts home in the evening." "Due not open this mail except Mr. Rosevelt." And simply, "Your letter openers better look out and not in."

Well, what does happen to your letter after you address it to the President at the White House and drop it in the mailbox?

Back in the McKinley administration when I first started handling the White House mail the answer would have been pretty simple. The postman would bring around a bag of mail, maybe a hundred letters, and I would open them and turn them over to the President's secretary or send them to one of the departments or to a stenographer for answer. Some of them I answered myself.

Today the principle is the same—but what a difference in operation! Before I retired as Chief of Mails at the White House in June of 1948, I headed a unit that had ten readers, twelve postal clerks, one assistant, one receptionist, two messengers, and myself to do the job I had once handled alone. And in rush times we had as many as seventy persons working to keep up with perhaps 150,000 letters, cards, and packages a day.

Mail arrives at the White House receiving room in a special sealed truck driven by a post-office employee who does nothing but deliver mailbags to the President. Your letter is buried somewhere in the pile of bags, but don't worry. It won't be lost.

A corps of clerks permanently detailed by the city post office to the White House takes over in the receiving room. They put the letters, which are tied in bundles, under a fluoroscope, a metal boxlike contraption about three feet by two and three feet high, and look at them through a glass window. If there is a dime or a paper clip or any other such object in your letter they will see it even if it is in the middle of the bundle.

They won't worry if they see either a dime or a paper clip, but if anything shows up that is puzzling or suspicious, the bundle is broken open and that letter is removed before the others are turned over to clerks in the sorting room. There are six sorting boxes where the mail is distributed to pigeonholes marked for the President, his wife, and various staff members. When a pigeonhole is full, the clerk at that position takes the letters out and stacks them up edgewise along his table. There is a ruler on the edge of the table, and he notes down how many inches of mail he has sorted for the President. Nobody counts letters to the President these days. They are measured by the foot or the yard, which gives the same result and saves time.

The mail for the President's wife goes to her secretaries, but the President's mail is stacked in piles on a long table. The Chief of Mails at the White House and his assistants go through these stacks to pick out the personal mail for the Chief Executive. You need a good memory for stationery, postmarks, and the itineraries of the presidential family, and you also have to be something of a handwriting expert to pick out the letters that go to the President unopened.

Another thing the Chief of Mails has to do is pick out what we called the "important" ones, which might come from anywhere. You soon learn, of course, to recognize the President's regular correspondents, but every mail brings its share of letters from political or business or foreign personages, and if one is missed or misdirected it might easily create a major crisis.

None of the nine Presidents under whom I served ever put a "hands off" sign on any correspondence addressed to him, except from members of his family or very close friends. After years of experience, it was not difficult for me to carry in my mind the color of stationery, the writing, the postmark, and other peculiarities that enabled me to pick out this personal mail. I could still recognize today the distinctive stationery used by the Theodore Roosevelt family, or the small silver-gray envelope that identified a letter from Mrs. Taft to her husband.

Mrs. Eleanor Roosevelt gave me the most trouble. When she was on a trip she seldom stuck to the advance itinerary, which we checked on regularly. Not only was it almost impossible to forward mail to her, but she wrote to the President from so many unexpected towns and on such odd hotel stationery that it was only with great difficulty that I could recognize her letters without opening them.

After sorting out the personal and "important" mail, the rest of the correspondence addressed to the President—probably including your letter—is run through the electric letter-opener, gathered in piles, and distributed to the readers, starting at about 8:15 A.M. A good reader can get through 500 or 600 letters a day, particularly if that includes a good many propaganda letters, which can be handled quickly.

The reader sees plenty of strange addresses on the letters that come to the White House. Many persons draw elaborate pictures or portraits of the President, or work out trick designs in the hope of attracting his attention. As has been noted, a typical stunt with T.R. was to draw a big stick on the envelope, with no other address, and with F.D.R. a picture of a rose was sometimes used in combination with the letters "v-e-l-t." But many of the addresses display the surprising ignorance—and sometimes the political sentiments—of the writers.

All such letters are acknowledged, but presuming your letter is a sensible one, it would get special attention, depending on the subject matter. Each reader must have a thorough knowledge of all the government departments and agencies and their duties, During the height of the New Deal alphabetical-agency period, that meant knowing plenty—usually more than anybody else in Washington knew or could puzzle out.

The reader has to decide at once what agency or department should handle each letter, and to be able to write the name or initials of that agency on the corner of the letter. Sounds simple, but it means knowing the names and duties of such agencies as FERA, HOLC, IEFC, CAA, ODT, NRA, WAA and ACPSAHMWA. You try to figure them out, and then remember that there were scores of them, and they were changing every other week. If you're curious, that last one was the American Commission for the Protection and Salvage of Artistic and Historic Monuments in War Areas.

On each letter the reader adds his own number (every reader is numbered) and then, on a prepared form, puts the name and address of the writer and a brief note of what the letter said and where it was sent. This is attached to the letter and sent to the filing room, where the prepared form is removed and filed and the letter is sent along to the correct agency.

The system of putting agency or department initials on letters once resulted in an amusing incident. A reader wrote AGR (for Agriculture) on a letter from a Midwestern farmer, and by mistake the letter was returned to the writer when it was answered. He saw the initials and, perhaps because there were a lot of peculiar questions asked in New Deal days, he got the idea that the letters were AGE and that we wanted to know how old he was. He wrote Mr. Roosevelt a letter saying that he didn't think it was any of our damn business, but if we must know he was sixty-two, and hale and hearty.

If your letter is to be handled or acknowledged by the White House staff, it is sent to the proper secretary or to the chief stenographer, perhaps after a memorandum has been filed regarding its contents. The important letters from Congressmen, businessmen, or perhaps friends of the President are opened by the Chief of Mails and his assistant and disposed of in the same manner, except that more of them find their way to the President or the secretaries.

So you can see that when you sit down to write to the President you're getting yourself involved in a lot of machinery, and the chances of the President's seeing your letter are about the same as a long shot in the daily double at Hialeah.

Nevertheless, the President does see a good many letters, and the summaries and other data that are supplied him make it possible for him to keep a close tab on public opinion and on the problems that are uppermost in the minds of ordinary people. In looking through my notes and records I am reminded that not all the "ordinary people" are Americans; that for many years the President received frequent letters from little people in other countries. One of them, a letter written in Tokyo on January 14, 1936, is a part of my records and it seems such a strange missive now—after the war—that it may be worth including.

Your Excellency
Mr. President and Mrs. Franklin D. Roosevelt

Since your Inauguration of presidency your candid policies proved much worth and improvement of general conditions can be seen to us a plain cityzen of Far East. We are highly respectingly congratulate you.

The world, all over quite uneasy trouble after trouble here and there. Unsteadieness, topling state only can be relzxed and let steady to safety through sincere, sympathetic understandings of each others situation, position. We are so believing.

1936 the year of election in your country. Political world becomes so active and bright. For the same policy and practition in America means not only for the countrys stability and steadfastness but also for the world at large. Each word actions movement of your Excellency directly reflect so nervously England rather

British Britain somewhat losing her former power while America gained whether she wish or not. The world affairs always somehow mingled because of her natinal power and being strong.

As a nation we think America is the best located and well provided by nature. Yet she must have her own natinal troubles, worries, problems, as any other powers. Especially at the present time. Your Excellency you need health, vigor and energy to stand for the heaviest responsibility ever fall upon a man.

We have red a book of biographies related chiefly upon American presidents. We were deeply toubhed, moved and we thought we could something for the president to relief his ever working brains and body. Let to be leisured whenever the chance to be. Our this Japanized english letter may interest your excellency's tired brain for change.

We also wish to present you a pure white woolen sweater to be wear when you have the opportunity for open air vacation, to comfort your body to please you. This sweater is designed and styled by me. Hand knited by my wife. We worked for completion together. Each day we took clean hot bath before our start and prayed as our own religious manner. Woolen yarn we chased English bee hive jumper 3 ply yars about the best obtainably in Japan. The measurement we were thought by our teacher. We hope our sincere devotion can be expressed within this sweater and will fit your excellency perfectly, smartly and suit to your taste.

We are sending this sweater to be honorably presented as a cityzen of Japan. A nameless plain business shop keeper is so vigorously and sincerely wishing an international good will and closer relation betterment of the either side of pacific countries even lasting co-existing and mutual progressions, prosperity, happiness and eventually the worlds' perfect peace and well faires.

We remain we are

Yours most respectedly
H. M. I——.
Ayako I——.

P.S. Please be kind enough to excuse us if using this plain paper and we wish your excellency to try understand this comical letter, the sort only you can receive, there are many errors mistakes but please help us to percive the bond of meaning We are much obliged and pray

The touching letter from the Japanese and his wife was followed some months later by notification that the sweater had been completed and dispatched, but for the life of me I cannot recall whether it ever reached the President.

So many gifts did arrive, especially at Christmas time, that they became a sort of blur in my mind except for a few outstanding items. I find in my records the following notation made on December 20, 1934:

CHRISTMAS SEASON MAIL

The regular routine letter mail continues at about 3800.

Christmas cards for the President and Mrs. Roosevelt are arriving in great numbers and will continue to increase until after the holiday. Today we handled about 2000.

Gifts for the President and Mrs. Roosevelt and other members of the family keep several clerks busy and will increase the work through Tuesday. The range extends from small, inexpensive, homemade gifts from obscure admirers to the more pretentious ones from personal friends. Fruit, a whole deer, ducks, pheasants, quail, nuts, jams, jellies, wines, and fish, as well as nine turkeys (one came express collect), canes, dolls, wood carvings, fancy sewing in the shape of quilts, pillowcases, handkerchiefs, etc. Picture frames, paintings, ship models, and old prints have been received.

A great many of the personal gifts come in care of Mrs. Roosevelt and are inspected and handled at the House.

In trying to give an idea of the volume and variety of work done in the White House mail room, especially during the last decade or so, I find that statistics are not really adequate. It seems to me that it might be more understandable and interesting if I made it possible for the reader to see the work done by one clerk in one day during the period of World War II, when mail volume was high. The following list is a record of letters handled by only one clerk in only one working day. The contents of the letters are indicated in the listing.

A request for deferment; a request for a job; 36 petitions against liquor and vice conditions around army camps; 4 letters urging freedom for Earl Browder; 1 letter opposing freedom for Browder; 42 more letters against liquor and vice around camps; a protest against inefficiency in government departments where clerks sit around idle and cause comment by men in uniform; a protest against drafting boys under nineteen; 11 invitations to high-school commencements; 6 clippings without names; an offer from a national organization to rally motorists back of the President's war leadership; 9 suspicious or crank letters sent to the Secret Service; a farmer's request for deferment; a proposal that Henry Wallace broadcast once a week; a poem; 2 letters asking release from the Army; an army private asks foreign service; a plan to speed the sale of defense bonds; praise for the FEPC; a plea to erase a man's prison record; thanks for a hospital grant; request from a Negro organization to interview the President; an inquiry re March of Dimes; a request for a birth certificate; a request for $1000 to finance an invention for national defense; a request for a patent; an idea for a motor to replace the gasoline motor; a man who caught two safe-crackers thinks he ought to have a reward; 4 letters re old age pensions; 61 petitions and 181 letters regarding morals and national defense; three suggestions of names for the Second World War; a prayer for peace; a protest against cigarette smoking; a letter re training of radio technicians; a request for the President's picture; a plan for price control; a plea for the release of a husband held by the F.B.I.; a study of Negro achievements in the Chicago public schools; 11 letters seeking deferments; a protest against widening a Washington street; a protest against gasoline rationing; a letter on the CIO; a protest against the excess-profits tax; 3 letters on racial discrimination; a request from a mother for permission for her fifteen-year-old daughter to take a job; a suggestion that 10 per cent of all salaries be invested in defense bonds; 2 requests to employ those over sixty in defense jobs; a plea to ban the sale of rubber tires to brewers; a suggestion that the Secretary of State be fired; a request for a presidential greeting at the dedication of a church; a request for an autographed photograph; an endorsement of a friend for work with the WPB; 2 offers of services in war work; a suggestion for special education of the people on government subjects; 2 letters saying to be sure and retaliate if the Japs use poison gas; a request for financial aid to develop a mine; 2 requests for less sugar rationing; an offer to give the Government a formula for an effective poison; an offer of an invention that seems to be a torpedo net; 3 letters from women seeking release of their husbands from the Army; an argument on the allotment of cotton acreage; a protest against the mobilization bill; a proposal to ban the use of copper except for defense; a plea to extend REA lines to farm property; a complaint that the Columbus, Ohio, general depot fails to deliver checks promptly; a demand for a second front; a letter on subversive activities; a request to help locate a husband; 4 requests for defense work; a request for automobile tires; a request for a patent on wooden car wheels; a proposal for an international conference; a protest against paying union dues; a request for information about a son in the Army; a proposal for a Congressional bill legalizing the marriage of white and colored persons; a plan for an airplane motor that does not use gasoline; a plan to speed delivery of lumber to defense projects; a plan for raising the morale of high-school boys, who are the "future soldiers"; a protest than men in army uniform are too attentive to a certain girl; a request that the Army draft a husband; 5 letters on price-fixing; 6 letters on gas rationing; 2 more poems; 3 more suggestions of names for the Second World War; a letter telling about troubles with the neighbors; a letter filled with political advice; a gift of toy rubber boots; a complaint about labor unions; a request for a post-office job; a proposal to sell a truck to the Government; a simple remedy for malaria; a request for money to pay for a wife's operation; an offer of an instrument for locating oil; 2 girls want to serve in the Army; 2 others want war work; a proposal that the Air Force bomb Japanese volcanoes; a request for a birth certificate; a letter of admiration for the President; a check ($23.30) for defense sent by school children; a pledge by a worker of 10 per cent of his wages for defense; a book of stamps ($18) for defense; 6 more suggestions of names for the Second World War; a proposal to seize Martinique and the Free French islands; an invalid asks financial backing for an original song; a proposal to ban the sale of fireworks; an offer of a girl's blond hair for precision instruments; an offer to sell a steel engraving of Lincoln; an outline of terms for a peace treaty with Japan; a patriotic poem; a schoolgirl's letter on what the U.S. means to her; a boys' club invites the President to be their honorary president; information as to a draft-dodger; a one-legged man wants a job or relief; an offer of an automobile headlight reflector to the Government; a charge that a husband fails to support his wife; a protest against the Eastern-seaboard blackout; 5 letters from Congressmen enclosing letters from constituents; a letter from G. Pinchot re lifeboat equipment; a suggestion about how to make liquor; a proposal to use the metal in post-office doors for defense; a request for money to launch a garden weeder; a sarcastic letter regarding the President's last speech; a letter to the President's dog; 5 patriotic songs; covers for a stamp collection; one more name for the Second World War.

This may seem like a long list for one man to get through in a day, but actually I have abbreviated it somewhat, since the clerk on that day handled a large number of organized-pressure letters that were all the same and didn't require careful reading. But to get an idea of the work the mail room did in these days, the list above would have to be vastly increased. The following tables, for instance, show the steady increase in mail over a period of three years, with January used as the sample month:

JANUARY 1942

| | *Letters* | *Cards* | *Misc.* |
|---|---|---|---|
| 2 | 2,905 | 175 | 1,810 |
| 3 | 1,635 | 110 | 1,285 |
| 5 | 2,045 | 360 | 1,305 |
| 6 | 1,610 | 140 | 1,085 |
| 7 | 1,840 | 120 | 1,270 |
| 8 | 2,035 | 110 | 1,170 |
| 9 | 1,685 | 50 | 1,120 |
| 10 | 1,820 | 75 | 1,115 |
| 12 | 2,810 | 185 | 1,570 |
| 13 | 1,755 | 130 | 935 |
| 14 | 2,870 | 125 | 1,335 |
| 15 | 2,410 | 130 | 1,115 |
| 16 | 1,685 | 100 | 910 |
| 17 | 2,830 | 110 | 1,435 |
| 19 | 3,285 | 210 | 1,115 |
| 20 | 2,055 | 85 | 745 |
| 21 | 3,415 | 105 | 1,110 |
| 22 | 4,510 | 170 | 1,205 |
| 23 | 4,085 | 125 | 1,115 |
| 24 | 4,015 | 195 | 865 |
| 26 | 9,430 | 385 | 1,935 |
| 27 | 6,115 | 175 | 810 |
| 28 | 13,110 | 160 | 1,055 |
| 29 | 15,880 | 190 | 1,310 |
| 30 | 22,665 | 160 | 1,235 |
| 31 | 22,570 | 310 | 1,105 |
| | 141,070 | 4,190 | 31,065 |

JANUARY 1943

| | *Letters* | *Cards* | *Misc.* |
|---|---|---|---|
| 1 | 1,215 | 25 | 785 |
| 2 | 1,535 | 35 | 1,025 |
| 4 | 2,115 | 130 | 1,435 |
| 5 | 1,270 | 55 | 985 |
| 6 | 1,580 | 65 | 995 |
| 7 | 1,535 | 80 | 1,015 |
| 8 | 1,720 | 85 | 1,115 |
| 9 | 1,745 | 70 | 1,045 |
| 11 | 3,080 | 125 | 1,340 |
| 12 | 1,440 | 130 | 865 |
| 13 | 1,985 | 255 | 1,020 |
| 14 | 1,815 | 175 | 1,015 |
| 15 | 1,740 | 245 | 985 |
| 16 | 2,105 | 215 | 1,035 |
| 18 | 2,570 | 335 | 1,165 |
| 19 | 2,065 | 150 | 785 |
| 20 | 2,515 | 245 | 880 |
| 21 | 2,935 | 310 | 855 |
| 22 | 3,655 | 205 | 930 |
| 23 | 4,090 | 470 | 885 |
| 25 | 8,435 | 385 | 1,440 |
| 26 | 10,065 | 205 | 840 |
| 27 | 15,575 | 140 | 990 |
| 28 | 20,200 | 180 | 910 |
| 29 | 20,770 | 140 | 845 |
| 30 | 26,300 | 230 | 835 |
| 31 | 24,110 | 250 | 680 |
| | 168,165 | 4,935 | 26,700 |

JANUARY 1945

| | *Letters* | *Cards* | *Misc.* |
|---|---|---|---|
| 1 | 1,770 | 275 | 1,250 |
| 2 | 1,070 | 70 | 615 |
| 3 | 1,165 | 65 | 920 |
| 4 | 1,640 | 135 | 1,120 |
| 5 | 1,620 | 225 | 1,275 |
| 6 | 1,540 | 55 | 920 |
| 8 | 1,810 | 150 | 1,435 |
| 9 | 1,425 | 80 | 1,070 |
| 10 | 2,620 | 160 | 1,515 |
| 11 | 1,820 | 225 | 1,270 |
| 12 | 2,545 | 215 | 1,275 |
| 13 | 2,735 | 95 | 1,140 |
| 15 | 3,115 | 175 | 1,505 |
| 16 | 2,545 | 45 | 985 |
| 17 | 4,140 | 80 | 1,465 |
| 18 | 5,840 | 90 | 1,710 |
| 19 | 7,140 | 110 | 1,445 |
| 20 | 10,440 | 125 | 1,735 |
| 22 | 16,035 | 145 | 1,720 |
| 23 | 9,040 | 160 | 1,085 |
| 24 | 12,985 | 215 | 1,315 |
| 25 | 14,750 | 1,010 | 1,340 |
| 26 | 14,987 | 630 | 1,265 |
| 27 | 19,765 | 375 | 1,235 |
| 28 | 14,400 | 380 | 1,015 |
| 29 | 23,070 | 510 | 935 |
| 30 | 18,330 | 445 | 775 |
| 31 | 30,070 | 590 | 1,270 |
| | 228,412 | 6,835 | 34,605 |

But the letters are just part of it. People also send packages to the President, and they are even more work. Later I will tell you just how they are treated. A lot of strange things came out of packages sent to the White House in the last fifty years; everything from gold teeth sent in by persons who heard it was illegal to hoard gold to the gold-plated toilet seat sent to Mr. Truman. When gold currency and coins were withdrawn from circulation, we received some $468,000 worth of gold articles from persons who misunderstood the Treasury order and believed that all gold articles had to be turned in to the Government. During World War II, many persons sent in contributions of money or gold articles to be sold for defense, ranging from $1 to buy bullets for use on the Japs to checks for $50,000 contributed by workers in a factory. All such contributions were sent to the Treasury.

Such gifts present many difficult problems. All of them are acknowledged, but few of them are anything that the Chief Executive would want or could use. Or if the gift is expensive, it may be refused because the President would find it unwise to accept anything that might put him under an obligation to the sender. All others, however, are kept for at least six months, no matter how useless or how horrible they may be. That rule was made after Margaret Le Hand, the personal secretary to F.D.R., received a package containing a statuette sent to the President. She found it so repulsive that she immediately shattered it. The sculptor later wrote in about it and we were involved in a six-months correspondence trying to explain why we couldn't either return it or pay him $200 for it. He finally got tired of asking.

The large number of gifts sent to F.D.R. resulted in the building a basement storeroom to hold the overflow of presents—some valuable and some merely horrible pieces of junk. This room was unofficially called "the Chamber of Horrors" because, as one newspaper reporter said, of the "grotesqueness of many of the goodwill gifts" received by the Roosevelts.

The reporter, J. Russell Young of the *Washington Star,* added that the President never used the term, but he had long since become aware of what was meant when he turned a gift over to a subordinate and the latter bowed out saying, "I will put it in the chamber of horrors, sir."

Young, a veteran White House correspondent, an amateur artist, and later a District of Columbia Commissioner, wrote a gentle and understanding article about the gifts that were sent to the Roosevelts, pointing out the desire of the givers to do something for the President and the First Lady, but also bringing out the problem that was created for them. The story said in part:

> Mr. and Mrs. Roosevelt, like most of their predecessors in the executive mansion, have followed a strict policy of returning all presents of any real intrinsic value. But, also like the prior occupants, Mr. and Mrs. Roosevelt have been happy to accept the many little and inexpensive remembrances and tokens of appreciation tendered them. They both make it a strict rule to acknowledge personally all gifts they feel they can keep.
>
> That, in itself, is something of a task when it is remembered the Chief Executive has many more pressing demands on his time. But, the real task is to find a place to put these gifts that are received.
>
> The White House is a commodious place in so far as homes go, but there is a limit to everything. The room originally assigned as the resting place for miscellaneous gifts during the early days of

the Roosevelt administration has long since been found inadequate. Another room in the White House is now catching the overflow.

In the President's old home at Hyde Park, N. Y., where he spends many week ends during the year, there also is a "chamber of horrors." The same is true of the President's little white cottage at the foot of Pine Mountain at Warm Springs, Ga. . . .

It is almost unbelievable what people really send to the President and Mrs. Roosevelt. There is no mistaking the fact that some of the articles have required great skill and deft fingers and many months of labor to execute. Most of the presents might well come under the classification of "junk," even though they are not treated as such in the presidential household.

To enumerate the many kinds of gifts would be like quoting from the pages of a mail-order house catalogue. In the matter of numbers, handmade neckties head the list. They come in all colors and styles, some embroidered and some knitted, many of them with the President's initials, some of them displaying a prominent "R" and some few of them bearing the President's likeness or what the sender intended as a likeness.

All sorts of wearing apparel are included in the list, socks and handkerchiefs being the most common. Then there are the many penknives, wood-carvings, wrought-iron work, water-color paintings and oil paintings, pictures in pastel or crayon, more frequently in pen and ink. As might be expected, most of these works of art are intended to be a likeness of the President. There are the fountain pens, pencils, stickpins, cuff links and shirt studs.

Following publication of a story a year or so ago about the President appearing at a banquet in evening clothes and wearing dark shirt studs intended for wear only on informal occasions, he was swamped soon afterward with white studs. This no doubt was due to the fact the President laughingly remarked when commenting on his improper attire, that he could not find his white shirt studs when he was getting dressed for the banquet. "I guess one of my sons helped himself beforehand," the President explained.

Peculiarly enough, the gifts are more or less of a seasonal nature. As is generally known, Mr. Roosevelt is susceptible to head colds. Each time stories are printed about him being indisposed the White House is flooded with presents from well-wishing friends in the form of handmade chest protectors, sweaters, wrist warmers, woolen socks and earmuffs, to say nothing of all sorts of homemade remedies for coughs and colds.

In the Summer the President receives a variety of homemade fans. Around Christmas there are many presents of homemade candy, fruits, cake, plum pudding and other delicacies identified with the season.

In the Autumn and Winter come the apples, pears, nuts, smoked hams and game birds, in addition to the customary number of turkeys received at Thanksgiving and Christmas time. There also are venison and bear meat, wild duck, pheasants and partridges, sent by proud hunters from various parts of the country. Then there are the various cakes and pies—the largest cherry pie in the world came by airplane from the Michigan cherry festival last Summer. Crates of oranges and grapefruit in great numbers are received. Some of these are prize winners in the citrus States. In addition, there are received quantities of fish, oysters, crabs and lobsters.

Ever since Mr. Roosevelt has been in office he has been the recipient each year of the first salmon caught in Maine waters. The best of the first seasonal tonging in Chesapeake Bay also are added to the White House larder.

The eatables, of course, are not sent to the "chamber of horrors." The articles which go to the President's table are carefully inspected and are either put in the White House larder for eventual use on the presidential table or sent to one of the local hospitals. But the handicraft—and some of it really is remarkable in its originality and execution—finds its way to the "chamber of horrors."

Some of these articles are on display in what is known as the "trophy room" on the basement floor of the White House, to be viewed by the daily visitors and sightseers. Most of the articles, however, are too crude to be put on display or be used by the

President or Mrs. Roosevelt. Therefore, generally after the President has examined them and made a notation of the name and address of the sender, they are relegated to the well-known chamber.

Just how often the "chamber of horrors" is emptied and what eventually becomes of the gifts, only one or two persons know and they are not revealing the fact. More than likely the President himself does not know. Certainly, the gifts are of no value either intrinsically or sentimentally. Very few of them have any real usefulness.

The fact is known that there is a "chamber of horrors"; that it comprises more than one room; that only a few people know exactly where it is, or how it operates. But it holds—and then gets rid of—the White House junk.

Gifts from abroad, normally, are accepted only if they come from foreign governments and can be made part of the permanent White House furnishings rather than the personal property of the President.

Each President is able to exercise considerable discretion regarding gifts, and there has been a good deal of variation. President McKinley was careful about accepting anything more than a crate of oranges or a box of cigars. Theodore Roosevelt received many odd gifts, especially canes in the shape of the "big stick" that he made famous, and his daughter Alice received a trainload of gifts when she was married. The Tafts accepted hundreds of silver gifts on their twenty-fifth wedding anniversary, as has been noted. Woodrow Wilson and Herbert Hoover were not interested, and did not want even the most inexpensive gifts, but Calvin Coolidge kept a close record of all presents, and took many of them home to Vermont when he left the White House.

F.D.R. received a tremendous assortment of gifts, with canes (because he was crippled) probably the leading item. He took an interest in odd gifts, little carvings, ship models, and trinkets, and littered the place with those that happened to strike his fancy.

Gifts coming in through the customs always cause a lot of trouble, but I believe it was most acute during the time of F.D.R. A typical example was a man in Panama who wrote to the President expressing his admiration, and saying that he had made a special deep-sea fishing rod and an exquisite reel, which he was sending as a gift. Miss Le Hand replied telling him that Mr. Roosevelt was very appreciative and was looking forward to using the equipment. A couple of weeks later the Collector of Customs notified me that he had a rod and a reel for the President. They had been appraised, he said, and the duty of approximately 50 per cent came to the neat sum of $480. Would the President, the Collector added, please send over the cash and he would send over the fishing equipment, which was handsome indeed. No cash, no rod or reel. I told Miss Le Hand and her mouth popped open.

"Oh, my!" she said. "I thought Panama was part of the United States. I didn't know there'd be any duty."

Neither one of us had any intention of asking the President to fork over the money, since he already had a truckload of fishing equipment. Miss Le Hand got together with the State Department experts on what to do and finally cooked up a letter to the kindhearted Panamanian. The President, she said, was not permitted to accept such valuable gifts, and therefore the State Department was forced to return the rod and reel. But, she added, Mr. Roosevelt was planning to make a voyage that would take him to Panama, and he hoped that the man would come aboard his ship and demonstrate the qualities of the equipment. He did make such a trip later and was primed to welcome the man, but he didn't show up.

After that, all letters regarding gifts from foreign countries were routed to me, and we investigated the question of duty and, when necessary, had the State Department send the gifts back with a diplomatic letter of explanation.

Winston Churchill crossed us up, however, when he returned the film of the motion picture *Woodrow Wilson,* which F.D.R. had lent him. It had been supposed that Churchill would send the film back in the British Embassy diplomatic pouch, which would not be subject to customs inspection, but he put it aboard a Cunard liner and there was no way to avoid the customs. I had to swear that they were for government use in order to secure them and give them back to the film company that had sent them to the White House in the first place.

President Truman received notice from the Customs Office at one time that a gift valued at $1000 had arrived for him. We checked up and found that it was a portrait of Mr. Truman that had been painted by the Latin American who sent it. It was either an esoteric masterpiece that I was unable to appreciate, or it was a rotten painting, and we so advised the President. He expressed a high degree of disinterest, and the State Department advised the sender that it was being returned because it was not proper for the President to accept such valuable gifts. They got a telegram back promptly saying not to send it back but please to sell it to somebody.

Mr. Truman always got a kick out of seeing presents or cards from his old friends. On one of his birthdays we were instructed to send all of the greeting cards to him. He evidently enjoyed seeing them, but we puzzled for weeks trying to acknowledge many of them with no other clew than a scrawled signature such as "Harry" or "Your pal Hank" or "Old Pete."

Once when the President made an offhand remark at a press conference about his own difficulties in getting white shirts during the war, he was inundated with a flood of white shirts in the next mail. Later, without saying anything, he received a lot of livestock from farmers who wanted to protest against the cost and the scarcity of feed. An Iowa farmer sent him a live hog that weighed 700 pounds. The $69 express charges were prepaid, and the animal was accompanied by a respectful letter saying the farmer couldn't sell the hog at a profit under current conditions—May, 1948—and was giving it to Mr. Truman. The President didn't have any place for a live hog, but the Bureau of Animal Industry agreed to take it. Their truck driver was happy when I told him the hog could be picked up at the Railway Express.

"Mr. Smith," he said, "I had visions of us chasing that hog all over the White House lawn."

"No," I told him, "that didn't bother me as much as the fact that we couldn't use him because he has no civil-service status."

A few days later Mr. Truman got another hog with another protest against the high price of feed.

During the Truman drive to save grain for Europe, a number of chicken farmers sent crates of live chickens to the White House as a protest against chickenless Thursdays. The letters accompanying them insisted, with tongue in cheek, that they were merely gifts to the President, but the real purpose was obvious. We finally had to get the express company to head them off at the express depot and deliver them to the Walter Reed Hospital.

The majority of gifts to the President are food of one kind or another. If a package of food was expected or came from someone well known—as when J. P. Morgan sometimes sent ducks to the White House—then we would inspect the package to see that there was no tampering, and sent it over to the kitchen. But otherwise we would send it directly to the Food and Drugs Administration laboratory to be tested chemically or on guinea pigs and monkeys. Most of the food was thrown away before the New Deal days, because there was no system then for testing it, and much of it arrived in poor condition.

The end of Prohibition brought one wave of gifts that I well remember. All the manufacturers were eager to get their products publicized, and we were buried under five-gallon cans of pretzels and bottles of legal beer. Three times a day the express trucks would bring a new load, and I was soon giving pretzels to anybody who would take them. The beer, for the most part, went over to the White House, but Mr. Roosevelt merely admired the freak bottles—some of them holding ten gallons—and declined to drink any. He had been drinking a home brew that was stirred up by Henry Nesbit, the steward, and he kept right on drinking it after Repeal. Said he liked it better.

The Presidents, with the possible exception of Mr. Wilson and Mr. Taft, have always been interested in the trend of the mail in so far as it indicates the swing of public opinion. In the early part of the century, when perhaps fewer than a hundred letters a day were received, people were not very well informed on the big issues before Congress. The newspapers carried less Washington news, there was no radio to spread word of what was happening in Congress, and only the most important problems were debated generally. The mail was slow, too. If you lived a long distance from the capital, it would take eight or nine days to get a letter to the President. By that time the problem at issue might already be settled or might have faded out. We probably got more telegrams than letters on an important occasion then, because they could be delivered quickly.

Very gradually, the whole situation began to change, and there was a great speed-up during World War I. The country now knows through newspapers and radio the details of governmental affairs, and with the aid of airmail the people let the President know what they think within a few hours. Much of this mail, of course, is the product of organized propaganda.

The first such pressure mail that I saw came from church organizations during the McKinley administration, and was concerned largely with keeping us out of war with Spain. It was customary then for religious groups to distribute leaflets in the pews of churches, suggesting that members of the congregation write to the President and giving an example of a letter that expressed the viewpoint of the group. We would get the first wave of letters from New York and New England, perhaps, but a week later we would be getting similar letters from the South and the Midwest, and then another wave from farther west, and probably it would continue for a month or two. I would soon be able to recognize such letters at a glance and would not bother the President or his secretaries with them, although they were kept informed of the number of letters received on each important issue.

In the Theodore Roosevelt administration, a coal strike brought a new twist in pressure. A number of newspapers printed coupons calling upon the President to force a settlement of the strike—there was then great need for reform in the industry and for the setting-up of safety standards—and readers were urged to send these coupons to the White House. They did at the rate of about 2000 a day. This deluge kept up for weeks, but after a short time I could tell by just feeling the envelope whether it was a coupon. Except for advising T.R. of the number received, I merely opened them and filed them away.

During the Taft and Wilson administrations, there was a stready growth in organized-pressure mail dealing with Prohibition and the events leading up to World War I. Organized labor, too, began bombarding the White House with letters, and in recent years labor probably has contributed more mail of this character than any other bloc. In June of 1947, the organized-pressure letters on the Taft-Hartley bill set a record, averaging about 18,000 a day. On June 12, for instance, we received over all 13,190 letters, 47,300 post cards, and 905 other items in the mail. This included 40,900 post cards demanding the veto of the labor bill.

That month of June was particularly heavy as far as pressure mail in general was concerned. A few statistics indicate what we had to deal with. On June 17 we received 3800 post cards on the Palestine question, 400 on lynchings, 4500 on Public Law No. 27 (barring foreign-born war-service seamen from American ships), and 10,900 calling upon the President to veto the Taft-Hartley bill.

Almost all of these were printed or mimeographed form cards that were distributed by various organizations to individuals who signed and posted them. The record of letters, cards, and other mail received for June was swollen as a result of these organized campaigns to the totals shown in the table on the following page.

I have never felt that such inspired mail amounted to much, but the Presidents have usually taken a different viewpoint. Some of them have been inclined to think that the dupes who write in on instructions represent the voice of the people, and all of them have wanted regular reports on such mail.

In 1948 there were fifteen different subjects under which records of pressure mail were filed. These ranged from civil rights to Prohibition to war with Russia. Letters and postcards of this type usually arrive in large batches. One delivery

JUNE 1947

| | *Letters* | *Cards* | *Misc.* |
|---|---|---|---|
| 2 | 8,770 | 21,800 | 705 |
| 3 | 3,110 | 6,900 | 635 |
| 4 | 5,440 | 12,600 | 735 |
| 5 | 9,270 | 17,200 | 635 |
| 6 | 10,140 | 18,600 | 775 |
| 7 | 7,670 | 15,600 | 605 |
| 9 | 21,015 | 61,000 | 1,235 |
| 10 | 10,140 | 18,400 | 680 |
| 11 | 11,380 | 34,400 | 675 |
| 12 | 13,190 | 47,300 | 905 |
| 13 | 12,600 | 37,600 | 910 |
| 14 | 6,170 | 13,900 | 635 |
| 16 | 12,370 | 44,200 | 1,005 |
| 17 | 3,175 | 11,500 | 610 |
| 18 | 4,775 | 20,400 | 705 |
| 19 | 4,050 | 10,900 | 710 |
| 20 | 3,510 | 9,600 | 770 |
| 21 | 1,510 | 3,700 | 505 |
| 23 | 2,615 | 3,650 | 840 |
| 24 | 1,065 | 1,000 | 505 |
| 25 | 1,310 | 475 | 735 |
| 26 | 940 | 535 | 540 |
| 27 | 1,040 | 970 | 535 |
| 28 | 985 | 350 | 580 |
| 30 | 1,375 | 650 | 575 |
| | 157,615 | 413,230 | 17,745 |

might bring 3000 letters on the same subject from, say, Chicago. Because they have all been written at the suggestion of a single organization and say about the same thing, they follow the same post-office channel, and are usually delivered in bundles containing about 300 each.

These are easily recognized by the experienced clerk, who reads the newspapers carefully and is probably expecting them anyway. They are thrown aside until the other mail is handled. Eventually, each letter is opened and a regular report is made on the number received and on the contents, in a general way. They are sent to whatever department is particularly interested in the subject, but a complete file of the names of the writers is cross-indexed in the White House offices—a practice started by Mr. Hoover and denounced by me ever since to anyone who would listen.

The whole problem of handling the White House mail has changed tremendously in the last twenty years, owing primarily to the huge increase in letters of every kind during the New Deal period. Prior to the arrival of F.D.R. at the White House, I had handled the entire mail by myself, except for some routine assistance in emergencies. This meant working holidays, Sundays, and until midnight on many occasions, particularly when a change in administration might bring 10,000 unopened letters in one week.

The inauguration of Mr. Roosevelt in the midst of the depression seemed to touch off the letter-writing instinct in most Americans. Or perhaps they had more time on their hands, and certainly they were worried. As already noted, when the President told them to write to him about their troubles they took him at his word by the hundreds of thousands.

"Dear Mr. President, I am worried about how we are going to . . ."

"Dear Mr. Roosevelt, The children have no shoes to wear to school . . ."

"Dear Frank, I've been driving a hack for ten years but now . . ."

"Dear Sir, Your detestable attempts to destroy our system of . . ."

They were all worried in one way or another, those who were down to their last yacht as well as those who saw the kids go to school with no breakfast, and they seemed to feel that they must let Mr. Roosevelt know their hopes and fears. They came in so fast we couldn't count them, but within a week I had some 450,000 unopened letters stacked all over the office.

I spent my entire time from 7:30 A.M. to midnight every day merely going through the stacks of letters and picking out those that seemed to be important. I put a couple of desks in a basement room that had a dirt floor and ran temporary lights into it, so I could get away from the office and work without interruption.

Finally, I took my problem to Rudolph Forster, the executive clerk, and he brought in the President's secretary, Louis Howe. I told them that unless they just wanted to burn the letters or throw them away we would have to have help. One man and one woman were brought in from other departments, but we soon decided that we would need a force of about fifty persons for a while.

That was not easy, when you remembered that capable persons would be needed, and the departments were reluctant to let good clerks go. The Civil Service Commission was unable to provide the class of clerks needed. Forster finally decided we could get help from outside the government service, and have them sworn in as employees of temporary agencies and detailed to the White House. There were plenty of capable persons out of work, or running elevators, in those days, and through my acquaintances I soon had hired twenty outside the classified service. They were happy to give up such jobs as they had and come to the White House. Then I heard from Forster again. He said in view of the President's position toward civil service he was afraid our action might arouse criticism, and that we should again try to get clerks through regular channels.

I blew my top. I told him these people had given up their jobs, and that I had given my word they would be employed. If I couldn't keep my promise, I said, I wanted him to get somebody else in my place.

"Now, Ira," he said, "don't be precipitate. If you've hired them, it will have to go through."

When it was all approved, I had the clerks, but nowhere to put them. We began expanding into the halls and other odd spaces, but still there wasn't room. It was decided to take over some space in the State Department Building across the street, and Colonel Edmund Starling of the Secret Service and I went over to discuss the problem. We didn't get very far, being turned away with the State Department's customarily diplomatic version of the run-around. We had to ask Mr. Roosevelt to direct that the rooms be commandeered, which he did.

That was just the beginning of our migrations, however. When the President decided to rebuild the excutive offices, we moved everybody over to the State Department rooms except myself and my assistant. We moved our desks and tables into the lower corridor at the east end of the White House, and worked there until the rebuilding was completed. Then we moved everybody back into the offices, and stayed there until President Truman ordered more rebuilding of the offices in 1946. Our entire staff was moved to some temporary army barracks behind the State Department, but no sooner had the move been made than Congress decided that the proposed rebuilding would mar the beauty of the White House, and withdrew the appropriation.

Our office, however, never did get back to the executive wing. We finally fought another battle with the State Department, which was as obstructionist and as supercilious as ever, in order to get suitable offices, and in June of 1947 we moved into the offices the Mail Department now occupies in the old State Department Building.

As usual we had to make a lot of special preparations there to handle the crank mail and to maintain the system for protection of the President from anyone who might decide to send him a package of high explosives through the mail. I want to tell about how that is done and about some of the queer ones we handled at the White House.

# CHAPTER THIRTEEN

EVERY PRESIDENT OF THE UNITED STATES, AS ANYONE KNOWS, must constantly face a limited risk of bodily harm at the hands of some crank or fanatic. But, as almost no one stops to think, the men and women around the President, and especially the Secret Service detail, must accept more or less the same risk, because they are just as vulnerable as he is to a bullet or a packaged bomb intended for the Chief Executive. I don't believe anyone around the White House has ever spent much time worrying about his own danger, and especially I don't believe any President has ever given it more than passing consideration. On the contrary, most Presidents have been scornful of the precautions taken by the Secret Service and it has been difficult for some Chief Executives and their families to understand quickly the necessity for such precautions.

This is often quite understandable. I remember, for instance, that Mrs. Eleanor Roosevelt was a bit slow to agree that it was necessary to continue our method of handling packages and gifts sent to the President. When I first went to her to discuss the mail problem soon after the arrival of the

Roosevelts in Washington, she was surprised that it would be necessary to examine all packages before they were delivered to the family. I pointed out to her the dangers involved in delivering uninspected packages to the head of a state, because some enemy might take advantage of such laxity to harm him.

"Oh yes," Mrs. Roosevelt said with a smile, "but everybody *loves* Franklin!"

"In that case," I replied, "it is difficult to understand whom Zangara was shooting at down in Florida last January when he killed Mayor Cermak instead of the President."

Mrs. Roosevelt agreed that it would be best if we examined the packages.

Since the beginning of World War II the measures for protection of the President have been the most elaborate and efficient that modern science could devise, but as I look back on my fifty years service in the White House, I often shudder to recall the risks that were run in earlier years. As Chief of Mails, I suppose I took my share of the risks, because cranks are just as likely to use the postal service as any other method of trying to get explosives into the President's office. Following the assassination of President McKinley, I was inclined to be suspicious of everything, and through the years I developed a sort of sixth sense in regard to packages that came unannounced in the White House mail. Sometimes I was right and sometimes I was wrong.

Many a time I prodded a package with a stick while holding an improvised shield in front of myself. Many a time I dumped a ticking box into a bucket of oil—often ruining a handsome gift clock addressed to the President. Many a time I wrecked the intricate model of some device sent in by an inventor who thought he was contributing a marvelous new weapon to our national defense.

It is no longer true, but until the time of Franklin Roosevelt the Chief of Mails had to depend largely on instinct and good luck and experience in handling dangerous packages, because we didn't have the elaborate scientific equipment that is now installed in the White House mail room. About the only good thing I can say about the old days is that at least I never lost a President.

There were, however, some occasions when I wasn't sure whether my luck would last. And there were times that were both exciting and amusing as the day in 1933 when I was opening President Roosevelt's mail and came to a package wrapped in brown paper and postmarked from Cleveland, Ohio. To the casual observer it would have seemed to be just an ordinary parcel, except perhaps for the scrawled address: "To the President of the United States." But to me it was an object of immediate suspicion. There was, I thought instinctively even before I had touched it, something wrong with that irregular handwriting and the sender's return address: "Lieut. Jenkins, Cleveland Police." When I picked up the package there didn't seem to be anything particularly unusual about it, but my suspicions were as strong as before. I held it out to one of my assistants.

"Buck," I said, "what do you think?"

He gave it a long look, shrugged, and said, "I'd rather you opened it."

I went over and checked the "lookout" file of letters that had come in telling us to be on the lookout for a package that would arrive later for the President. There was nothing in regard to Cleveland or Lieutenant Jenkins. I decided to try a method I had developed for opening suspicious packages backward.

The normal way to open a package is to cut along the top, or to untie it and loosen the folded paper. That is also the way to touch off a bomb in some cases if one happens to be inside the package. A crude bomb, for instance, might have a match placed so that it will be ignited by friction when the paper is loosened, to touch off gunpowder, which in turn will explode the bomb. My system was to open the suspicious packages in as nearly as possible the opposite manner.

In this instance, I started cutting a hole in the bottom of the package. Under the brown paper I found a stiff cardboard box, and looped through the sides of the box I discovered many small copper wires. That was enough for me. Any package that ticked or had wires inside always got my goat—and with good reason, too. I decided to give Lieutenant Jenkins's package the full-dress treatment.

My first move was to go to the lobby outside the President's office, where, as I had expected, I found the inimitable Colonel Edmund W. Starling, chief of the White House Secret Service detail, resting comfortably on a divan.

"Colonel," I said, "I think I've got something of interest to the Secret Service."

The Colonel was not a man to pass up the dramatics in any situation. He sat up, tightened his rugged jaw, and narrowed his eyes at me. I told him about the package. He made a quick but safe decision.

"Let's soak it," he said.

We took the parcel out into the back yard of the White House, got a bucket of water, and dumped it in. Then we went about our business. Twelve hours later we got a couple of long sticks from the basement and fished the package out of the bucket. Using the poles like elongated chopsticks, and ready to hit the deck at any moment, we began tearing the package to pieces.

We smashed the box and disclosed yards of thin copper wire wound back and forth in an intricate pattern through a queer-looking lump in the middle of the package. We sweated and prodded some more, and didn't seem to be getting anywhere. Finally I threw down my pole and stepped closer to the mess.

"You know what that looks like?" I asked Starling.

The Colonel shook his head irritably, suggesting that he didn't much care what it looked like. He was getting good and tired of Lieutenant Jenkins's little parcel.

"It looks," I said, "like a sweet potato."

We took a closer look and it *was* a sweet potato. The Colonel personally confirmed it with a fine outburst of disgust. He bundled the whole works up carefully, with the idea of trying to trace the sender.

"Well," he said as he stalked away, "we made a noble effort—however futile."

There was nothing in the package but the wires and a harmless sweet potato. All efforts to trace what must have been a man with a distorted sense of humor failed. We never knew the answer, but it was a long time before we could see anything even faintly amusing in the incident. My only solace was that I had been right—there was something wrong with that parcel.

The sweet-potato "bomb" was just part of a day's work, but we never knew when we might come across something far more serious, and we never took chances. And we had some queer experiences with cranks and with some characters who meant real danger, especially when they followed up their letters or packages with visits to the White House.

One of the crackpot variety who crashed the White House back in the McKinley administration was typical of the mental cases who seem harmless enough but might at any time become fanatical and dangerous. This fellow arrived carrying a bundle made up of branches and weeds, with a Bible nestled in the center. He insisted that he had to see the President. If he did not, his bundle, which was really a voodoo creation, would bring about many horrors, including the ousting of Mr. McKinley and the election of a king. He could prevent these catastrophes, he added, by explaining to the President that the branches he carried represented various political groups, and that some of them had to be lopped off. The whole situation could be saved, he went on, by eliminating William Jennings Bryan from politics—an idea that would doubtless have appealed to Mr. McKinley had it been proposed by anyone but a voodoo doctor.

A more amusing incident occurred when Mr. Coolidge was President. There was a wealthy real-estate man in the Midwest who became well known to us because he was always writing to the President on important issues, about which he apparently knew nothing. Finally he showed up at our office, confident that the President would be pleased to see him.

By that time I had a good idea of his eccentricities, and I told Everett Sanders, the President's secretary, that I didn't believe he should be received by Mr. Coolidge. Sanders, however, checked up and found that the caller was a wealthy man, and he remained on the engagement list. I then went around to Dick Jervis, head of the White House Secret Service detail, and told him it would be a good idea to keep his eyes open.

The gentleman arrived and was taken to the door of the President's office at the appointed time. Everything was going fine. But as he stepped forward to shake the President's outstretched hand the silence was broken by the tinkling tones of music boxes, a cascade of pleasant but startling little tunes that seemed simply to emanate from the person of the visitor. Mr. Coolidge stepped back quickly behind his desk, aghast. Jervis pounced.

When they got the fellow back in our office—still without shaking hands with the President—he began taking little music boxes out of every pocket of his suit. They were beautiful golden boxes, which, he said proudly, cost $400 each. He lined them up on a desk and played them for the clerks, pleased with the attention he was getting. He didn't, however, get any attention from the President. Mr. Coolidge was not amused.

Another strange case centered around an old German who lived in New York. He wrote to the President in German on many occasions, and there was an intriguing childlike simplicity about his letters. I always read the translations carefully, especially after he began telling us about his domestic troubles in letters that were like installments of a soap-opera serial. He had found a young girl almost starving on the street and had taken her home. Apparently he mistook her gratitude for love, but in any event they were married. Then after a short time his letters said the girl had started looking around for youth and fun. Finally she left him. It was a terrible blow to the old man, and it was clear from later letters that it preyed on his mind constantly. His business was neglected, and it failed. He walked the streets. He was hungry. He was a bum, and he still wrote to the President about it.

One day he appeared at the White House, and since I knew about his letters, I talked to him through an interpreter. He said he had been sitting in the park across the street, hungry and tired and not daring to come to see the President. He wandered, dazed, into a restaurant and somebody asked him a question. He didn't understand, but he answered "*Ja*" and they brought him some ham and eggs and coffee. After eating, he got up enough nerve to come in and tell us that his wife was persecuting him and he wanted the President to help him. I told him that the President had given orders that he was to be looked after. Following the usual routine, he was sent to St. Elizabeth's, as he was obviously a mental case by that time. He was pleased and grateful. When I went there later on other business, he rushed up to shake my hand

and thank me for the magnificent accommodations the President had given him.

On several occasions persons who had written to the President and then followed up their letters with visits to the White House were so far off balance that they threatened to act violently, but we usually had police help at hand to subdue them. There was one Rumanian-born citizen who wrote to President Hoover in regard to the handling of our relations with Rumania. He didn't like the way things were going, and he made various proposals for improvement, all of which were so wild that we were very much on the alert when he finally showed up in person.

I arranged for assistance to be nearby when I talked to him. He was impatient, and wanted to see Mr. Hoover, but I explained that the President was so busy that an interview could not be arranged. I pointed out all the clerks in the office and said that it was their duty to relieve the President of some of the burdens of office. Suddenly our visitor's attitude changed. He said he agreed with me. He shook hands warmly and departed. The next week he was back.

"I just dropped in to shake hands," he explained. We shook hands warmly. He was very jolly. He came in about once a week for several months and we shook hands. Finally, after a warm shake, he showed me a passport visaed for Rumania. He said he was going back there to see what could be done from that end, and I guess he did, because I never saw him again.

One other intriguing case lasted for many years. President Theodore Roosevelt received a letter from an American woman who was married to a European Count, saying that the United States Ambassador at one of the European capitals had, because of jealousy, blocked her presentation at court. She wanted the Ambassador fired. She didn't get any satisfaction, but she kept on writing long letters to the President, and we formed the opinion that she was suffering from some delusion. Anyway, nothing was done other than to refer her letters to the Department of State. Then one day she turned up at the White House and wanted to talk to the President. When we heard that she had arrived, we were merely amused, but when she came into the office we could only stare at her. She was one of the most beautiful women I have ever seen, and she was dressed as if she had just stepped from the pages of a fashion magazine.

One of the President's secretaries took a look at her and left the lobby at a rapid pace, explaining that he was afraid that if he talked to her he would end up by giving her the United States Mint and joining the royalist party. A newspaper reporter who knew the story of her letters refused to write about her, because he said he would be sure to end up with an editorial backing her complaint. She finally departed without seeing the President and without achieving anything but an office sensation, but we kept on getting letters from her for years. The Ambassador retired. Mr. Roosevelt was out of office and finally died. There were wars and revolutions. But the Countess kept right on writing to the President, always with the same complaint.

We were frequently reminded that so-called crank cases could be full of political dynamite. One such case concerned the unbalanced wife of a Congressman. She demanded that the President prosecute some absurd claim against her husband, and finally had to be led, screaming and struggling, from the office by two policemen. She later publicly charged that she had been thrown out of the White House, and newspapers all over the country published her story, permitting the administration's political foes to make capital of the case.

The White House is always the target of so many cranks that it is sometimes difficult to know when the President might be in real danger. Crude bombs made of lead pipe have been found in the White House mail, but they were comparatively easy to detect and destroy. Sometimes, however, we were lucky enough to recognize less obvious explosive packages.

In the Hoover administration, we received a slim little box addressed to the President, but with no indication of the name of the sender. I didn't like the looks of it, and I opened it backward, finding a fountain pen inside. I still thought it was peculiar that anyone would send Mr. Hoover a fountain pen without identifying himself, so I put it to soak in oil. Later I unscrewed the ink receptacle instead of taking off the cap of the pen. Inside the rubber ink container was a high explosive. When I unscrewed the cap, I found the oil-soaked head of a Fourth of July sparkler and a sprinkling of powder, so placed that it was intended to cause an explosion when the cap was unscrewed.

We were always suspicious of packages that did not carry the sender's name or address, and especially of gifts of candy.

We could test most food packages, but candy was destroyed unless we could be sure of the identity of the sender and knew that the package had not been tampered with. I always worried about gifts of liquids, too, and kept only those that could be tested. That meant I had the sad duty of destroying a lot of champagne, because even with scientific methods I have never found a way of testing champagne without opening the bottle and therefore ruining the wine.

The number of threatening letters to the Presidents has had little to do with the personality of the Chief Executive. In bad times there is likely to be an increase, as during the last part of Mr. Hoover's administration. Presumably this is due to worries that cause more and more persons to resort to extreme measures. One of the common types of threatening letter, for instance, is from some person who states his own desperate economic plight and says that unless "something is done" to solve his personal situation he will commit an act of violence.

There was a sharp renewal of crank letters after the start of World War II, largely sent by persons with fanatical views on international affairs. This trend continued after the death of F.D.R., and Mr. Truman received threatening letters as a result of intense feeling over postwar foreign developments. Nobody could guess which threats were the work of mere cranks and which might be serious, but as usual no chances were taken. Fortunately, we were tipped off to a lot of letters before they were received and the Secret Service was able to keep watch on the senders or to take further action if necessary.

It is not uncommon for some responsible citizen to advise the White House that he has learned of a threatening letter that is being sent to the President, or that he has heard about a threat to the safety of the Chief Executive. One letter in the nature of a warning, but perhaps merely the work of a crank, was forwarded to us by the mayor of a large city. It said that an attempt would be made on the life of President Truman at the Army-Navy football game. It is customary at the game for the President to sit on the Army side of the field during one half and on the Navy side of the field during the other half, walking across the gridiron between halves. That walk, the letter said, would be the last walk ever taken by Mr. Truman.

The Secret Service could not relate the letter to any previous crank communications, but of course took the most elaborate precautions. Men were stationed at frequent and strategic spots in the crowd and on the field. Mr. Truman crossed the gridiron between halves with a smile and a confident step, but a lot of other men close to him didn't breathe easy until the game was over.

On another occasion, in the summer of 1947 I was summoned back to Washington from my vacation because controversy over important issues, including the Palestine question, had greatly increased the volume of mail to the President. I was rather surprised that the volume should be more than could be handled routinely by the office but when I got back I found that not all the difficulty was due to volume. Some of the letters received had obviously been intended to kill.

There had been a flurry in England in June of that summer

because eight or more government officials and political personages had received terrorist letters in which explosives were cleverly concealed. Among those who got such letters were Foreign Secretary Ernest Bevin, Colonial Secretary Arthur Creech Jones, President of the Board of Trade Sir Stafford Cripps, and former Foreign Secretary Anthony Eden. Cripps's secretary noticed that the letter he received was hot (police said later it was apparently about ready to explode) and he stuck it in water. Eden carried his letter unopened in his briefcase for twenty-four hours before a secretary, tipped off by police, found it. There were two envelopes, the outer one about eight by six inches and cream-colored. The innner envelope was marked "Private and Confidential," presumably in an effort to see that it was opened by the man to whom it was addressed. Inside the second envelope was powdered gelignite, a pencil battery, and a detonator arranged to explode when the envelope was opened. Police exploded one experimentally and said that it was powerful enough to kill a man. The so-called Stern gang of Palestine terrorists later claimed responsibility for having sent the letters from its "branch in Europe." The letters were postmarked from Italy.

The same kind of terrorist letters had been found in the White House mail, and as a result the staff had been handling all letters with great care, thus slowing up the routine. So far as I know none of those received in this country resulted in an explosion, which may have been due to the excellent system introduced for handling the White House mail during the war.

This system makes full use of all modern scientific methods. When it was installed after consultation with many experts, the Secret Service turned over to me a fluoroscope and an x-ray machine, and arranged for clerks in the receiving room to be trained in the technique of handling explosives. As has been said, all food packages, unless their origin was favorably known and there was no possibility of tampering, were ordered sent to the Food and Drug Administration laboratory, where scientific tests were conducted before any package was taken to the White House kitchen. Various tests were made, but in most cases the laboratory would try out the food on animals and send back a report such as the following, dated August 20, 1947:

"Reference is made to your letter of August 18 submitting for examination approximately one half bushel of peaches. Two peaches were fed to two monkeys with no ill effects. Inspection of the fruit with a hand lens revealed no evidence of tampering. The remaining peaches were delivered to your messenger today."

Even the food that is purchased daily for the White House was placed under special supervision. Secret Service men pick up all groceries that are ordered, and they watch the butcher while the meat is being cut. They then carry the food purchases to a special truck, lock it in, and deliver it directly to the kitchen.

The general run of packages received in the mail includes a large number of queer ones, most of which are turned over to the Secret Service for possible inquiry. In running through my records, I find notes like these:

Received Nov. 20, 1944: small package addressed to the President containing old labels from tin cans, old letters, and post cards. The Secret Service and Office of Protective Research have a file on the sender.

June 23, 1947: A large letter, addressed to the President, was received. It contained a smoking pipe, three boxes of safety matches, a bunch of feathers, and three stones.

Nov. 29, 1946: Two recordings received from New Orleans. The recordings give an incoherent speech pertaining to Moses, Representative Sol Bloom, birds, etc.

Sept. 10, 1943: Received a parcel containing the works of five alarm clocks and several pieces of metal from Meridian, Miss."

Oct. 7, 1947: Received a package containing a $10 bill. Writer states that she heard Lincoln's letter read and thought perhaps it was a hint that the President needed money.

All packages that come in the White House mail are examined under the fluoroscope, which shows up any dense material, particularly metal. If we do not know in advance what the package contains, any parcel containing metal, especially clockworks, is put under the x-ray. This may show sufficient detail to prove that it is harmless. But if after examination by the bomb detection experts it is found to be dangerous, the package is turned over to the Secret Service and placed in a specially built bomb trailer.

The trailer looks like a huge urn, and is constructed of twisted wire cables and mounted on two wheels. The heavy cables never have been tried with an atomic bomb, but there is no question that they are strong enough to withstand a very powerful explosion. The trailer is then attached to an armored car, an extremely heavy vehicle built of steel and with portholes for machine guns. The bomb or suspected bomb is then taken to a special testing ground, where final disposition is made by the Secret Service experts. The details of bomb disposition are the business of the Secret Service, and I would not want to discuss their methods in any way that might interefere with their operations. The disposition, however, is quite definite and permanent.

The routine handling of crank letters is also highly developed now, and the Secret Service is likely to become acquainted with the writers in a hurry. When such a letter is found by one of the staff that reads the White House mail, it immediately goes into a special category, which includes any letter that is threatening or obscene, or suggests that the writer is mentally unbalanced.

The reader marks it for the Secret Service and puts his own initials on it. It is then stamped—both the envelope and the stationery—in the dating machine, and placed in a large cellophane envelope without folding.

These letters go to the Office of Protective Research, which is a branch of the regular Secret Service under the Treasury Department and has its offices in the east wing of the White House executive office. There each letter is photographed, processed, analyzed, and indexed. This means that the letter is checked for fingerprints (other than those of the staff reader, which are on file), the handwriting is studied, and a record is made of all the characteristics of the letter.

About half of such letters are anonymous, but in any event the characteristics of each are checked against an elaborate file to see whether it is a first letter or a repeater. If it is a first letter and if it is only mildly annoying, it is unlikely that any action will be taken. The letter is merely filed for future reference. But if it is a repeater or a particularly threatening letter, a photostat probably will be sent to a field agent in the community from which it is postmarked. If the writer has signed his name, the Secret Service usually contacts him or his relatives and secures a promise (often broken) not to write again.

But if the writer is anonymous, the Secret Service usually can chase him down, especially if he is a repeater. One man who had lost his job in a paper mill and wrote threatening letters to Mr. Hoover was trailed on an automobile trip from Cleveland to the West coast and back through the Northern states to Chicago, dropping a trail of letters all the way. He managed to keep one jump ahead of the agents until he got to Chicago, where the trail seemed to end. The Secret Service didn't stop, however. They checked every paper mill in the area, found a man who seemed to meet their description, trapped him into writing a note the handwriting of which matched that of the threatening letters, and arrested him.

Perhaps three or four letters a week are received at the White House from persons who either directly threaten the President or have heard dangerous talk against him or who say they are in such desperate straits that unless the President helps them they will kill themselves. In such instances, telegrams are sent at once to the nearest Secret Service field agent, giving him full information, or referring to previous letters if the writer is already on file and therefore well known to the field agent. The agent then moves in with the aid of postal inspectors, local authorities, and whatever other agencies are available.

Of course sometimes the Secret Service fails to locate an anonymous correspondent. One woman in Santa Monica, California, wrote a number of letters to President Truman. They were literate and neatly written letters, but they threatened Mr. Truman with various unpleasant fates. The woman seemed likely to be harmless, but she was a persistent soul, and the Secret Service hunted her in vain for months. Never did find her. Or at least they hadn't found her up to the summer of 1948, when I decided that fifty-one years was enough time for one man to devote to opening the President's mail. There'd been quite a few times between 1897 and 1948 when I was a bit fearful that somebody would retire me involuntarily, but in the end I made it under my own power.

I had been planning for some time to retire and to live in California, but I found it difficult to break away from the scenes that had been so familiar for so many years and from the many person who were such loyal friends and coworkers. The evolution of the White House mail-room staff had been slow, and had proceeded partly by trial and error, but by the time of World War II it was an excellent and efficient group, and gradually I found myself in a strictly supervisory position. The atmosphere inside our office was pleasant and the work went along smoothly, with ten skilled clerks from the city post office and twelve employees who read the mail and performed other duties.

On the fiftieth anniversary of my service in the White House I was surprised by the staff, who arranged a party for me in the office. In the morning President Truman had sent for me and reminded me that the date was March 26, 1947, and that I had become the first person on the White House rolls to complete fifty years of continuous service. I knew it before the President told me, but it was pleasant to hear him say it and to have him call in the photographers when he presented me with a photograph inscribed: "Kindest regards and congratulations on his fiftieth year of efficient service to Ira Smith from Harry Truman." I didn't know, however, what was waiting for me back at the office. When I returned there, I found an assembly of secretaries, officials, workers, and friends, and we all had a very merry time.

When I officially requested retirement later—early in 1948—I said that I intended to live in California, and we planned to leave Washington for good in the summer of that year. When this became known, there were lots of friends who wanted to give farewell parties for us, and for a while I doubt that the Government got its money's worth out of me at the office, because I was always gadding about.

Several days before my departure from the office for good, I noticed there was considerable secretive scurrying-around on the part of the staff, and sure enough on Saturday there was a really wonderful party. One of our messengers, calling himself Piccolo Pete, had organized an orchestra that provided the music, and about two hundred old and new friends came into the offices, which had been gaily decorated for the occasion.

There was a buffet luncheon and a bit of ceremonies, over which Bill Hassett, one of the President's secretaries, presided with great charm. In behalf of the office personnel, he presented me with numerous gifts, including a traveling bag and a deep-sea fishing outfit. There also was a book in which each member of the White House staff had written and to which the President added a few words. I think everybody attended the party except the President, who was down on Chesapeake Bay for the week end, but he sent me a letter which said:

> Dear Mr. Smith,
>
> A man who has served his government faithfully and well through more than fifty-one years has indeed earned honorable retirement. I cannot allow you to leave our White House staff without this word of appreciation for the efficient manner in which you have discharged the exacting duties which have fallen to you as Chief of Mails.
>
> We have all benefitted from your expert handling of the distribution of the enormous volume of mail which is the daily quota at the White House. May I express my particular thanks for the uncanny way in which you have been able to segregate my personal and family letters from the great mass of correspondence which has gone through your hands day after day.
>
> Hope you enjoy life to the fullest where the fishing is good.
>
> Very sincerely yours,
> Harry Truman

I thought that was pretty nice of Mr. Truman, especially that part about the fishing. I think that sometimes a man has to live in the White House for a while to realize how important fishing is to the enjoyment of life to the fullest.

I was pleased, too, when Mrs. Ethel Haberkorn, who had joined our staff in 1933 and later became my assistant, took over as Chief of Mails upon my departure. I knew that she had ability and initiative and would do a good job. I worked up until noon of my last day, but there were newspaper and radio and television people all over the office and I guess I didn't really get much done before we got into our automobile and headed for California.

It gave me a nice, warm feeling, leaving the White House that way instead of having it suggested that it was time to go, which, when you come to think of it, is the thing that any President normally has to face sooner or later. It was especially pleasant to receive Mr. Truman's congratulations and to be the guest of honor at the farewell parties, and to be reminded that I'd witnessed from the White House about one-third of our country's entire history.

I hadn't seen much of Southern California since I was a boy and lived on the ranch in the mountains near Santa Ynez, but I'm getting another look at it now. There are thirteen lemons on the little tree I planted in the yard behind my house at Santa Barbara and next year the oranges should be large enough to eat.

There is only one rule that is enforced at our house these days. My wife has to open all the mail.